Seasons of Splendour

Seasons of Splendour

Madhur Jaffrey

Seasons of Splendour

Tales, Myths & Legends of India

Illustrated by Michael Foreman

ATHENEUM   *New York*   *1985*

THIS BOOK
IS DEDICATED TO
THOSE WHO INSPIRED IT
PREM BHUA, KIRAN BHUA,
SHAMMO BHUA AND BAWA

First American Edition

ISBN 0 689 31141 9

Filmset in Great Britain by BAS Limited
Originated and printed in Italy by Arnoldo Mondadori

Contents

Dear Reader,

When I was about five years old, there was a roll-top desk in my uncle's study. Between its four legs was a space that seemed enormous and quite perfect for putting on plays. With a few old sheets tacked on as curtains, we had an ideal stage.

We wrote the plays, my cousins and I.

You see, we all lived together in my grandfather's large house in Delhi. There were a good five dozen of us, a strange mix of short, plump women who spent their days pickling, cooking, knitting and gossiping, tall shrewd men who went to work every day in gleaming cars and returned to play bridge and drink whisky, old servants who polished the cars, milked the cows, mowed the grass and put up the mosquito nets, and a lot of cheeky children who spent much of their free time either listening to stories told by the elders or else translating them into live theatre. Presiding over this entire brood was my white-bearded, barrister grandfather.

There was no tradition of bed-time stories in our family. Perhaps our parents, aunts and uncles just did not want to yell out stories to twenty bedded-down children.

No. Our family tradition of story-telling consisted more of the family huddle. We would crowd around an aunt on the Big Room divan or around my grandmother on the Prayer Room carpet or, if my mother was telling the story from a drawing room sofa, we would drape ourselves over its arms and back, even overflowing onto the floor, bodies overlapping bodies.

The fund of stories seemed endless. The plump women of the house would no sooner emerge from their baths in freshly starched summer voile saris, their faces smelling of powder and vanishing cream, than we would drag them to a sofa or carpet or divan to tell us a story. They would demur, we would insist. They would give in and settle down langourously with a great rustling of their crisp saris. Pillows would be adjusted. One leg would be tucked under the other. Soon there would be no sound other than the whirring of the fan and the twittering of garden birds.

'Since Lord Krishna's birth is about to be celebrated, how about the story of his birth?'

'Yes, yes, yes,' we would say in unison.

'Could you go up to the point when Krishna slays the serpent?' a cousin would ask.

'Please make the wicked King Kans really, really wicked,' I would add. 'Could we have red bulging eyes?'

Some of the stories we were told were of ancient origin and were drawn from our religious epics. Others, also ancient, had no recognizable source. They had just been told, in my family, generation after generation for centuries. What all the stories had in common was a clear moral tone. This made it more comfortable for the elders to tell them to us and, strangely enough, it made us children feel secure. What was right and what was wrong was so very clearly defined.

Death, however, was never hidden. As in our lives where those who died were kept at home until the family could place them on biers and carry them to cremation grounds for the final ceremony, so in our stories death was always treated as a part of the cycle of life—as much an open, family matter as birth. Children were born at home and the old died at home. I was born in my grandfather's house in a back room that overlooked the Yamuna River. Years later my grandfather died in the same house in a front room overlooking the garden. The stories that we were told were designed not only to separate right from wrong but to prepare us, indirectly, for the vagaries of life and the fact of death.

We, as children, did not know all this, of course. To us the stories were just plain fun.

In the heat of the afternoon when the elders of our house, well stuffed with lunches of pilafs, kormas and pickles, would stretch out on large divans for the afternoon nap, their last words to us as eyelids drooped were, 'Try to sleep. You need rest. Whatever you do, do *not* go out in the sun.'

I am afraid we did go out. But we heeded our elders to the extent that we stayed in the shade of the mango or tamarind tree.

It was here that we told *our* stories. One cousin might tell the story of *A Midsummer Night's Dream* that he had seen as a school play, another might regale us with an episode from the adventures of Robin Hood.

The next step was to put together all our new information in the form of a play to be staged under that roll-top desk, for the delight of our adoring and very indulgent parents.

What sort of plays did we make up?

We were children of two completely different cultures. I, for example, had a mother and grandmother who could not speak a word of English and who told me stories that reinforced my ties to my Hindu, Indian past. The schools I went to were either Catholic convents or Anglican missionary schools where all subjects were taught to us from English text books as if we were sitting in a small school in Cumberland. India was still a colony so I was learning 'Little Miss Muffet', 'Half a pound of tuppenny rice' and, many years later devouring *Jane Eyre* and *Great Expectations*.

I knew vaguely that the poems and stories at school were different from the ones my mother told me. But I did not really know why. Nor did my cousins.

The result was that when, on those summer afternoons we met under shady trees to write our plays, our conversation would go like this:

First cousin: 'Why do we not stage the fight between the good King Ram and the demon King Ravan?'

Me: 'Could I play Ram?'

Second cousin: 'No, you are a girl.'

Me: 'It is only a play.'

Third cousin: 'Why do you not play Ram's wife, the good queen, Sita?'

Me: 'But Sita does not *do* anything. She is only, well, good.'

Fourth cousin: 'Can you shoot a bow and arrow? I can. I should play Ram.'

Me: 'I could learn. I have almost learned cricket.'

First cousin: 'Let us get on with it. Up to the time Ram is banished to the forest, events are quite clear. We will follow grandmother's story. When Ram reaches the forest, why do we not arrange to have him meet Robin Hood and his Merry Men who have also been banished to the forest?'

Me: 'Yes, yes. Then Friar Tuck can assist the monkey god Hanuman in finding the kidnapped Sita. I will play the demon king, Ravan, who kidnaps Sita.'

Fifth cousin: 'No you won't. You are a girl. When Ram meets Robin Hood, could he say "Well met by moonlight, proud Robin Hood"?'

And so it would go. We hardly understood the differences between East and West. We just assumed that Someone's grand plan included all of us in it, with all our differing cultures.

What follow are some of the stories that were told to us by the women of our household. They were always told, not read. I doubt if a good half of them have ever been written down. Some, like the story of Doda and Dodi, are possibly unknown outside my family.

I have arranged the stories in sequence as they might be told at religious festivals during the course of a Hindu calender year. We use the lunar calender and our year starts at the time of the Spring equinox around mid-April. It is the 'moon-day' on which tradition says each story should be told.

I hope you enjoy the stories.

My very best to you,
Madhur Jaffrey

P.S. If you are going to read the stories aloud and need help with the pronunciation of proper names, please turn to page 125.

THE DAYS OF THE BANYAN TREE

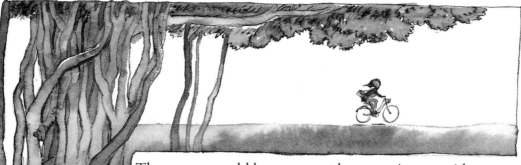

There was an old banyan tree that grew just outside our house. It was more than a tree, it seemed to be a whole forest, all by itself.

Its trunk went up, up, and up, almost a hundred feet. Some of the branches, instead of rising and spreading like outstretched arms, made nose dives towards the earth, where they burrowed in, took root, and reappeared as fresh trunks. My nanny—or *aya*, as we called her—said that the roots of a banyan tree went all the way to the Underworld and that when they rose again as fresh trunks, they carried up with them all sorts of ghosts and goblins. She insisted that there never was a banyan tree without a few ghosts lurking in its branches.

I believed her.

My grandmother, on the other hand, said that the banyan tree was a blessed tree because it had the wisdom of its years and because it provided so much shade. In fact, in the burning months of May and June, we prayed to it and offered it the best of the summer's yield—seedless cucumbers, watermelons, aubergines and mangoes.

I saw my grandmother's point. In the summer, scorching winds blasted in from neighbouring deserts carrying with them particles of sand to irritate eyes and parch throats. When the sky overhead felt like an oven with its door left open by some careless cook, the banyan trees offered cool, natural arbors to perspiring travellers.

My grandmother always advised me, 'On your way back from school, remember to get off your bicycle and rest under the shade of the banyan tree.'

Rest under the banyan tree and bump into a ghost!

Oh dear me, no! I paid no attention to my grandmother. In fact, when I reached the banyan trees, I held my breath and bicycled for my life.

No ghosts were going to catch me!

Here are two stories that were told on the days of the banyan tree. One on a moonless day in May, the other on the seventh day of the waning moon in June.

Savitri
and
Satyavan

ONCE UPON A TIME there lived a King and Queen, who after many years of being childless, gave birth to a daughter.

She was the most beautiful baby the parents could have hoped for, and they named her Savitri.

When Savitri grew up and it was time for her to marry, her father said to her, 'Dearest child, we hate to part with you. You have given us the greatest joy that humans can ever know. But it is time for you to start a family of your own. Is there any man you wish to marry?'

'No father,' replied Savitri, 'I have not yet met a man I would care to spend my life with.'

'Perhaps we should send for pictures of all the nobles in the country. You might come upon a face you like,' said the King and he sent his court painter to bring back portraits of all the nobles and rulers in the country.

Savitri examined the portraits, one after the other, and shook her head. The men in the portraits all looked so very ordinary, even though they were all emperors, kings and princes.

The King then said to his daughter, 'It might be best if you went to all the big cities of the world to find a husband for yourself. I will provide you with the proper escort of men, elephants, camels and horses. Good luck. I hope you can find a man to love.'

Savitri set out with a large procession of men, elephants, camels and horses. In her effort to visit all the cities of the world, she had to cross many oceans and deserts. She did this fearlessly. But she never found a man she could love.

When she returned home, her father said to her, 'You have looked in all the big cities of the world and have found no man that you wish to marry. Perhaps you should now search through all the forests of the world.'

Savitri set out again with a large procession of men, elephants, camels and horses, and began searching through all the forests of the world. She did this fearlessly.

She had looked through the last forest and was just about to return home when she came upon a young man who was cutting wood.

'What is your name?' she asked.

'Satyavan, your highness,' he replied.

'Please do not address me as "your highness",' she said, 'my name is Savitri.

What do you do for a living?'

'I do nothing much,' the young man replied. 'I have very old, blind parents. I live with them in a small, thatched cottage at the edge of the forest. Every morning I go out to cut wood and gather food. In the evening I make a fire for my parents, cook their dinner, and feed them. That is all I do.'

Savitri returned to her father's palace and said, 'Dearest mother and father. I have finally found a man to love and marry. His name is Satyavan and he lives in a cottage by a forest not too far from here.'

'But will you be able to live a simple life in a simple cottage?' asked her father. 'This young man obviously has no money.'

'That makes no difference at all to me,' Savitri said. 'He is capable, honest, good and caring. That is what I respect and love him for.'

The King sent a message to the blind couple's cottage saying that Princess Savitri wished to marry their son, Satyavan. When Satyavan arrived home that evening with his heavy load of wood his parents said, 'There are messengers here from the King. Princess Savitri wishes to marry you.'

'I love the young lady in question,' replied Satyavan, 'but it will be impossible to marry her. She has money, jewels, elephants, camels and servants. What can I offer her?'

Tears rolled down the faces of his blind parents. 'Son,' cried the mother, 'we never told you this, but long ago, before you were born, your father too was a ruler with a kingdom of his own. His wicked brother blinded us and stole our birthright. You should have been born a prince and heir to the kingdom, quite worthy of the beautiful Savitri. We have fallen on hard times, but if you two love each other, why should you not marry? Who knows what the future has in store for anybody?'

So a message was sent back to the King saying that Satyavan had agreed to the match.

On the day of the wedding, the King and Queen held a huge reception. Everyone of any importance was invited.

That is how it happened that the wisest Sage in the kingdom appeared at the scene.

Just before the wedding ceremony, the Sage took the King aside and whispered, 'It is my duty to warn you. The young man your daughter is to marry is decent and of good character, but his stars are crossed. He will die very shortly. This marriage would be a tragic mistake.'

The King felt ill when he heard this. He called his daughter and told her what the Sage had said, adding, 'Perhaps it is best to call the marriage off.'

'No, father,' Savitri said solemnly, 'I will marry Satyavan, whatever our future may hold.'

Savitri was no fool, however. She had heard that the Sage knew of heavenly remedies for earthly problems.

'Oh dearest Sage,' Savitri said to him, 'surely there is a way I can prevent my husband from dying. You, in your great wisdom, must offer me some hope.

There must be something I can do?'

The Sage thought deeply, 'You can extend your husband's life by fasting. Eat nothing but fruit, roots and leaves for a year, and Satyavan will live for those twelve months. After that he *must* die.'

With a sense of doom hanging over the bride's family, the wedding did take place. The groom and his parents were told nothing of what the future held for them.

Savitri began to lead a simple life with her husband and parents-in-law. Early each morning, Satyavan set out for the forest to cut wood and to forage for food. When he was gone, Savitri made the beds, swept the house, and shepherded her in-laws around wherever they wished to go. She also prayed and fasted.

One day Savitri's mother-in-law said to her, 'Child, we know how rich a family you come from. Since we have lost our kingdom, we can offer you no fineries but Satyavan does collect enough food for all of us. We have noticed that you eat just fruit, roots and leaves and never touch any grain. That is not a healthy diet. We are beginning to worry about you.'

'Oh, please do not worry about me,' begged Savitri. 'I love to eat fruit.'

The twelve months were almost over. On the very last day, Savitri got up with her husband and announced that she would accompany him into the forest.

'Child, what will you do in the forest? The work is hard and there are all kinds of dangerous animals,' said her mother-in-law.

'Do stay at home,' said Satyavan, 'the forest is not a comfortable place.'

'I have travelled through all the forests of the world. I was not uncomfortable and I was not frightened. Let me go with you today.'

Satyavan had no answer for his wife. He loved her a lot and trusted her instincts. 'Come along then, we'd better start quickly. The sun is almost up.'

So they set out towards the heart of the forest.

Once there, Satyavan climbed a tree and began to saw off its dried-up branches.

It was a scorchingly hot day in May. The trees had shed the last withered yellowing leaves. Savitri looked for a cool spot to sit down and just could not find any. Her heart was beating like a two-sided drum. Any moment now the year would end.

'Ahhh . . .' came a cry from Satyavan.

Savitri ran towards him, 'Are you all right?'

'I have a piercing headache.'

'Come down from the tree. It's the heat. I will run and find some shade.' Savitri found a banyan tree and helped Satyavan towards it. Many of the banyan tree's branches had gone deep into the earth and come up again to form a deliciously cool grove. The leaves rustled gently to fan the couple.

'Put your head in my lap,' Savitri said to Satyavan, 'and rest.'

Satyavan put his head down, gave a low moan, and died.

Savitri looked up. There, in the distance coming towards her was Yamraj, the King of the Underworld. He was riding a male water buffalo, and Savitri knew that he was coming to claim Satyavan's soul. She turned to the banyan tree and implored, 'Banyan tree, banyan tree, look after my husband. Shield him and keep him cool. I will return one day to claim him.'

Yamraj took Satyavan's soul and started to ride away. Savitri followed on foot. She followed for miles and miles. Yamraj finally turned around and said, 'Why are you following me, woman?'

'You are taking my husband's soul away. Why don't you take me as well? I cannot live without him.'

'Go back, go back to your home and do not bother me,' Yamraj said.

But Savitri kept following.

Yamraj turned around again, 'Stop following me, woman,' he cried.

Savitri paid no heed to him.

'Well, woman,' said Yamraj, 'I can see that you are quite determined. I will grant you just one wish. As long as you do not ask for your husband's soul.'

'May my in-laws have their sight back?' asked Savitri.

'All right, all right,' said Yamraj, 'now go home.'

After several more miles Yamraj glanced back. There was Savitri, still following.

'You really are quite persistent,' Yamraj said. 'I'll grant you one other wish. Just remember, do not ask for your husband's soul.'

'Could my father-in-law get back the kingdom he lost?' Savitri asked.

'Yes, yes,' said Yamraj, 'now go, go.'

Several miles later, Yamraj looked back again.

Savitri was still following.

'I do not understand you. I've granted you two wishes and yet you keep following me. This is the last wish I am offering you. Remember, you can ask for anything but your husband's soul.'

'May I be the mother of many sons?' Savitri asked.

'Yes, yes,' Yamraj said. 'Now *go*. Go back home.'

Several miles later Yamraj looked back only to see Savitri still there. 'Why are you still following me?' Yamraj asked. 'I having already granted you your wish of many sons.'

'How will I have many sons?' Savitri asked. You are carrying away the soul of the only husband I have. 'I will never marry again. You have granted me a false wish. It can *never* come true.'

'I have had enough,' Yamraj said. 'I am quite exhausted. Here, take back your husband's soul.'

Savitri rushed back to the banyan tree so her husband's body and soul could be joined again.

'Oh banyan tree,' she said, 'thank you for looking after my husband. In the years to come, may all married women come to you and offer thanks and prayers.'

Satyavan opened his eyes and said, 'My headache has gone.'

'Yes,' said Savitri, 'thanks to the kind banyan tree that offered us its shade. Let us go home now where a surprise awaits you. I will not tell you what it is.'

Satyavan put his arm around his wife's shoulders and they began to walk slowly back home.

Shravan Kumar
and
his Wife

SHRAVAN KUMAR was an upright young man. His wife, however, had traits in her character that were, at best, questionable. She was not completely bad, but she often came close to being so.

She treated Shravan Kumar's parents very badly. They were old and blind and lived with the young couple. Shravan Kumar's wife not only resented this, she showed her resentment by doing some rather nasty things.

For example, she kept two cooking pots in the kitchen. In one pot she made delicious sweet puddings for herself and her husband. In the other pot, she made sour puddings for her parents-in-law. The poor parents-in-law went on eating whatever they were given, but one day they said to their son, 'Son, we hate to complain. The fact is, we are quite tired of eating sour pudding every day. Could we possibly have something else to eat?'

Shravan Kumar could hardly believe what he heard. Whatever was put on his plate was always so delicious. His wife was a good cook.

That day at dinner, he exchanged his plate for his father's—and got a nasty surprise.

'Ugh!' he cried. 'What foul stuff is this?'

It was then that he discovered that his wife kept two pots in the kitchen, one for them and one for the parents.

'Wife,' Shravan Kumar said next morning, 'what you have been doing is not a good thing. From now on all the food for our family must be cooked in one pot.'

'Yes, dearest husband,' his wife replied meekly. She really *did* want to be good. It was just so very difficult for her, and it was easier to be mean.

Shravan Kumar's wife went to a potter and said, 'I have a special order. I need a clay pot with two stomachs, right away.'

'With two stomachs?' said the bewildered potter.

'Yes, yes, two stomachs. It is not so hard. Just put a division in the centre. Start right away.'

'Whatever you wish, madam,' said the potter, and he proceeded to make Shravan Kumar's wife a pot with two stomachs.

That night at dinner, Shravan Kumar smiled benignly at his parents. His food was delicious. As all the food was cooked in the same pot, he was sure his parents' food was just as good.

The parents said nothing for a few days. Then, they called their son aside and said, 'Son, we hate to complain. The fact is, we are quite tired of eating sour pudding every day. Could we possibly have something else to eat?'

Shravan Kumar could hardly believe what he had heard. That day at dinner, he again exchanged his plate for his father's.

'Ugh!' he cried. 'What foul stuff is this?'

It was then that he discovered that his wife had a pot with two stomachs.

'Wife,' Shravan Kumar said next morning, 'what you have been doing is not a good thing. I am upset and disappointed in you.'

'Dearest husband,' his wife replied meekly, 'I am really sorry for what I have done. From now on I will serve the same food to all of us.'

This time Shravan Kumar's wife was determined to be good.

'Your fine intentions will have to wait for a while. My parents are very old and I fear that they will not live long. They have asked me to take them on a pilgrimage. I intend to start out right away.'

'May I come too?' asked the wife.

'No, it is best if you stay at home. You see, I want my parents to enjoy this trip. If you come with us . . .'

He did not need to finish his sentence. His wife's head drooped with shame.

'I will stay at home, then, just as you wish,' Shravan Kumar's wife said. 'When you return you will see how good I can be. How will you travel? Your parents are too old to walk or ride on horses.'

'I have made two large baskets and attached them to the two ends of a pole. I will seat one of my parents in each of the baskets. I will sling the pole across my shoulders. That is how I will carry my parents to their place of pilgrimage.'

'You are such a good son, I will try to be a worthy wife.'

That day, Shravan Kumar set off on a pilgrimage carrying his old blind parents in the two baskets.

It was June and the sun was blistering all it threw its light on.

Shravan Kumar's parents said, 'Son, let us stop and rest. Besides we are very thirsty.'

Shravan Kumar put his parents down and left them to rest in a shady grove.

'The River Saryu is not far from here. I will go and fetch some water for you to drink.'

Shravan Kumar walked to the river and just as he was bending to get water, he was struck by an arrow and mortally wounded.

It was King Dashrat who was out hunting and who mistook Shravan Kumar for a deer.

Shravan Kumar began to cry out in pain, 'Oh, God, help me.'

When King Dashrat heard these cries, he ran towards his quarry and begged his forgiveness.

'There is no time to talk,' Shravan Kumar said, 'just . . . ease out the arrow . . . my parents are thirsty . . . they are blind . . . they were going on a pilgrimage . . . take them some water and tell them what has happened to me. Look after them.' Shravan Kumar became unconscious and lay dying on the ground.

King Dashrat took the pot of water and went searching for Shravan Kumar's parents.

The parents had been waiting in the shady grove wondering what had happened to their son. When they heard footsteps, they cried out with joy, 'We are so glad you are back. Come and rest, son, you must be tired.'

'I am not your son. I am King Dashrat. I was hunting deer and my arrow accidentally hit your son. I'm deeply sorry for this. Your son sent this water and has asked me to do whatever you desire. I am your servant.'

Tears began to fall from the blind eyes of both parents.

'Our son's accident is more than we can bear. Death is approaching fast and we are ready for it. Make us a funeral pyre and when we are dead, lay our bodies on it. That is all we want from you.' Then they cursed King Dashrat, 'We hope you are parted from your beloved son one day and die from the pain of it.'

King Dashrat built a funeral pyre of sandalwood and when the parents had died, he put them on the pyre and cremated them just as a son would have done.

The King then set out to find Shravan Kumar's wife and tell her the news.

The wife said, 'Tell me where he is.'

'You will find him lying on the banks of the River Saryu.'

Shravan Kumar's wife rushed to the River Saryu where her husband lay unconscious with a deep wound in his back where the arrow had pierced it.

It was another scorching day and there was nothing near the river but sand and scrub. If the wound did not kill her husband, the heat surely would.

Shravan Kumar's wife scanned all directions. She finally spotted a tamarind tree:

> 'Tamarind tree, tamarind tree
> Will you give us some shade?'

'Not I,' said the tamarind tree. 'Look elsewhere.'

The wife cursed the tree saying, 'May your fruit always be sour.' Then she ran toward the neem tree:

> 'Neem tree, neem tree
> Will you give us some shade?'

'Not I,' said the neem tree. 'Look elsewhere.'

The wife cursed the neem tree. 'May your fruit only be good for the treatment of boils and pimples,' she said, running toward the banyan tree:

> 'Banyan tree, banyan tree
> Will you give us some shade?'

'Come,' said the banyan tree, 'take refuge in my cool arbors.'

Shravan Kumar's wife dragged her husband into the shade of the banyan tree. There she sat with his head in her lap, weeping and weeping.

The great old banyan tree finally took pity on the poor woman. 'You have not been perfect,' the banyan tree said. 'You were cruel to your parents-in-law, but as a wife you have done better. And you seem truly remorseful. I will restore your husband to you.'

So saying, the banyan tree dripped healing milk into the wound and Shravan Kumar was cured.

His wife was cured too. She was never mean again.

A SPECIAL BIRTHDAY

All of India worships the blue god, Krishna. My feelings for him have always been a bit more personal. Not only was I raised on the banks of the Yamuna River, as he was, but I was born on the feast day of his birth—the dark, eighth day of the waning moon in August when monsoon winds, often laden with thick pellets of water, knock on all the doors and windows of Indian homes. On that day, we celebrated two birthdays, his and mine. While the Yamuna River never parted for me, as it did for Krishna, I did learn to toddle on its sands, to throw my first fishline from its rocky shore, and to swim in its unclear waters.

In the winter, the Yamuna River was too cold for swimming. Only the fittest young men with well-oiled bodies took the plunge. In the monsoon season it was swollen and too dangerous, what with deep, swirling whirlpools and treacherous currents. It was in the summer, early in the morning and early in the evening, that it was just perfect. My cousins and I would roll up a fresh set of clothes into towels and in a large, chattering group, walk towards the river.

'What stroke do you want to learn?' a ten-year old cousin once asked me. He was the swimming champion at school and double my age.

'Any stroke will do,' I answered as if I knew what strokes were.

'Well, first you learn how to float and then I'll teach you how to crawl. Now, lie flat in my arms and keep your head down.'

'Shall I keep my eyes shut?'

'As you want.'

I kept my eyes shut. It was not so easy to float.

'Wait,' said my cousin.

He swam to the far shore. I saw him walk up the sandy bank and disappear in the watermelon fields. Soon, he could be seen rolling a large watermelon towards the river. As soon as it hit the water, the giant fruit began to float. 'Hang on to the watermelon with your arms outstretched,' my cousin said. 'Keep your head down and kick your legs without bending your knees.'

That did it. I was held aloft by the watermelon and carried downstream by the gentle summer current. From the nearby temple came the sound of hymns sung to the accompaniment of conch shells. I was *almost* swimming.

I wonder if Krishna, the blue god, learned to swim in the same way?

The Birth of Krishna, the Blue God

Once upon a time there lived a wicked king called Kans, who ruled over Mathura, a kingdom that sprawled on the banks of the Yamuna River.

He should not have been king at all, for the real ruler was Kans's father, but he languished in a dungeon where his wicked son had put him.

Kans had a sister called Devaki, a sweet, gentle girl who had reached the age of marriage. Kans approached his sister one day and said, 'Devaki, I have arranged a match for you with a young, handsome man called Vasudev. He is of noble parentage and very wealthy. Your horoscopes match perfectly. The marriage will be good for you, good for Vasudev, and will prove quite beneficial to this court.'

The wedding took place as planned, but just as Devaki and Vasudev were about to leave for their new home, a wise man appeared at Kans's elbow and whispered, 'Do not let this couple go. Do you not know that you are doomed to die at the hands of their child?'

Kans went wild with fury. He pulled at Devaki's hair, drew his sword, and was about to cut her head off when his chief minister intervened, 'Your majesty, why commit the crime of killing your sister on her wedding night in full view of all the guests? Would it not be easier to throw—quietly of course—the couple in prison? Then, as and when the children are born, we can dispose of them. No one need know what is going on.'

Kans agreed to the plan. Devaki and Vasudev were thrown into prison where they became quite devoted to each other.

In time, Kans received the news that Devaki had given birth to a baby daughter. He sneaked into the prison through the back door. 'Where is the child?' he thundered as he entered the cell. Before Devaki could let out a yell, he had picked up the baby and thrown it to the ground.

The baby, instead of just lying there, turned into a bolt of lightning that zig-zagged upwards towards heaven, calling:

'Kans, you have done an evil thing
But I am not the one you seek
My brother is yet to be born
He will come and kill you.'

Six other daughters were born to Devaki. Kans came and killed each of them and as he did so each turned into a bolt of lightning that zig-zagged towards heaven, calling:

'Kans, you have done an evil thing
But I am not the one you seek
My brother is yet to be born
He will come and kill you.'

It was on the eighth day of the waning moon in August, and the monsoon raged outside the prison cell. Vast armies of thick black clouds marched across the skies, accompanied by drum-rolls of thunder. The rain poured and poured. Roads were turned into rivulets and rivers into seas.

On such a dark, dark night, yet another baby was born to Devaki. It was Krishna.

No sooner did he let out his first little cry, than Vasudev, his father, heard a voice from heaven saying, 'Now, now. Take the baby now. Take him to Gokul across the Yamuna River and exchange him for your sister's newborn daughter. Return before dawn and all will be well.'

'But the locks . . . the guards . . . the swollen river. . .' Vasudev hesitated.

'Have no fear,' said the voice.

Vasudev wrapped the newborn baby in the few rags he could lay his hands on. When he got to the cell doors he found that they were open and the guards around them were sleeping.

He carried the baby Krishna past the cell door and out into the wet street. When the lightning crackled overhead it gave a brief flash of light. Otherwise, he was surrounded by the deepest darkness.

At last Vasudev came to the banks of the Yamuna River. The monsoon rains had changed its gentle summer character so that it was now like an angry ocean, roaring in the darkness. Whenever the lightning flashed all Vasudev could see was water. Nothing but water, its surface stirred up into huge waves and nasty, circling whirlpools.

Vasudev had no choice. The baby had to be taken across the river to Gokul if his life was to be saved.

He put Krishna into a threshing basket and tucked the basket firmly in the crook of his right arm. Then he waded in.

Vasudev could hardly believe it. The water seemed to be rising even as he walked. He transferred the basket to the top of his head, but the water rose higher. Soon it was up to his nose.

What the poor human father did not realize was that the river was rising only because it wished to touch the god Krishna's feet.

The baby knew this. Very gently he lowered a tiny foot so it dangled down from the basket, low enough to touch the water. At once the mighty Yamuna River receded and parted, making a path for father and son. As they crossed the river bed the waters closed behind them.

In Gokul, Vasudev made straight for the house of his sister, Yashoda. There he exchanged his son for his newborn niece, then returned to his cell just the way he had left it.

Next morning, Kans got word that Devaki had given birth to yet another daughter. Again, he sneaked in through the back door and snatched the baby up to kill it.

But this time, the baby girl flew right out of his hands crying,

> 'Kans, you intended to do an evil thing
> But I am not the one you seek
> He is born already
> And safely tucked away.'

Kans was furious. He raved at Vasudev and Devaki for deceiving him. He yelled at the gods, 'I will get the boy. You wait. He is not getting away from me. Nobody defies King Kans.'

Kans issued a royal decree that would take care, once and for all, of his little enemy: all newborn males in the kingdom were to be put to death.

The King's soldiers went forth—into every little hut and every palace—and they slaughtered every male child that was under twelve months of age. The parents screeched and cried but Kans was immune to their pain.

He laughed in his palace.

Finally, he was secure from all threats to his life.

What he did not know was that Krishna was not in his kingdom at all. Gokul lay outside his domain. The baby Krishna was safe.

Krishna
and the
Demon Nurse

THE WICKED KING KANS thought he was sitting securely on his throne when an informer approached him one day with these words, 'Your highness, I notice you are feeling very happy these days.'

'And why should I not be?' asked Kans. 'There are no rebellions in my kingdom, my enemies are quiet, and there is enough gold to last us for several generations.'

'Your father still languishes in prison, so there is no threat there.'

'Yes, yes,' said Kans, dismissively. He did not wish to think about his father too much.

'There is one problem, as I see it,' the informer went on.

'And what is that?' said the King, suddenly wary.

'Devaki's son.'

Kans stood up. 'Get out of my sight. How dare you bring up such matters.'

'Well, if you do not want me to talk about it . . . I have nothing to lose by being quiet. I will say no more.'

'What on earth are you trying to tell me?' Kans thundered.

'Do not listen to me if you so wish. All I came to tell you was that Devaki's son. . .'

'Devaki's son is dead. All male infants were killed on my orders,' Kans said.

'Apparently not all. Not this one. He was taken across the Yamuna River, outside your kingdom, outside your realm and there he lives—in safety. He is being brought up by foster-parents, his aunt, Yashoda, and his uncle, Nanda, the cowherd. He is still a baby, of course . . . something can still . . . be arranged. I understand that the family is looking for a nurse.'

'Are you sure of your facts?'

'Oh yes, I have checked them very carefully. Krishna is definitely Devaki's son.'

'I know what I'll do,' said Kans, who excelled in thinking up evil schemes. 'Go and find the demon, Pootana, and bring her to me.'

Pootana was never easy to find. She was always running around the world on unpleasant errands of her own, but the informer managed to locate her at the bottom of a well where she was making a meal out of toads.

'Hey, Pootana,' the informer yelled down the well, 'King Kans needs you. Come up and I will tell you about it.'

'Is it dirty work he needs me for?' Pootana yelled back, 'Otherwise I'm not coming.'

'Yes, you know King Kans well enough. Simple killings he leaves to his soldiers. This errand requires your special skills.'

Pootana liked flattery. 'Wait, I'm coming up,' she yelled back.

What came creeping over the wall of the well was a sight to behold.

Pootana was ugly and smelly.

Her black, pimply face had two small eyes peeping out from tiny openings and out of her mouth protruded two large fangs.

Pootana followed the informer into the presence of King Kans.

Kans held his nose, struck anew by the odour that Pootana gave off.

'You do smell very bad!' Kans said.

'Have you called me here to insult me? If so, I shall leave.'

'No, no, stay. We have business to conduct. There is a baby . . . a boy called Krishna in the household of Nanda and Yashoda in the town of Gokul.'

'And that town is outside your kingdom.'

'You guessed correctly.'

'But there are other means. . .'

'And that is where you come in. Now, if you walked into that cowherd's house in Gokul looking as you do they will not let you in.'

'I can disguise myself,' snapped Pootana.

'I know, I know. I want you to become the prettiest, sweetest, most soft-spoken, loving damsel possible. Dress modestly and try to get the job of nurse in that household. Once you are in, find a way of killing the child. Take your time and be careful. That family seems very shrewd. Here are some jewels for your pains.'

'Consider the job done,' said the demon as she crept away.

The very next day, a sweet, gentle, shy girl appeared on Yashoda's doorstep. 'I hope I am not disturbing you,' the girl said.

'Oh not at all, please come in,' Yashoda said in her friendly way.

'Actually, I came here because . . . I'd heard you had need of a nurse . . . I . . . I . . .,' the girl could not go on. She fainted on the doorstep.

Yashoda sprinkled water on her forehead and put some quilts over her to warm her up. It was January now. The baby Krishna was almost six months old.

Slowly the girl came to. 'Oh, I am such an inconvenience to you. It is just . . . that I have not eaten for a few days. There is a famine in my village . . . and my entire family . . . my husband and children . . . have perished.'

'Oh dear,' Yashoda said. 'I will get you some food right away.'

'Please,' said the girl, 'I don't want your charity. I would really like to pay for my food with work. Perhaps you can employ me as a nurse for your son. I miss my own children so very much.'

'Oh yes, that is perfect,' Yashoda said. 'Why not? I am sure you will be a kind nurse to our son.'

And so Pootana was employed as a nurse in Nanda and Yashoda's household.

She was careful, just as she had promised King Kans. For weeks on end she appeared as a real nurse. She cooed to the baby, played with him and made him laugh.

'You seem to have found the perfect nurse,' Nanda said to his wife, Yashoda.

One day when Yashoda was running a fever Pootana said to her, 'You rest. Why don't you let me feed the baby instead. I have plenty of milk in my breast.'

'Very well,' said Yashoda, who now trusted the nurse completely. 'I'll just sleep for a bit. I'm sure that will make me feel better.'

Pootana took the baby into a back room. First she put poison on her nipples, then said to the child, 'Come now, baby, here's your food, suck. . .'

Krishna was no ordinary baby. He took her nipple firmly between his gums and sucked and sucked. And sucked and sucked. And sucked and sucked.

'Stop, you are hurting me,' Pootana said pushing the baby's mouth away.

But the baby would not be pushed away—and he would not stop sucking.

Pootana began screaming and dancing wildly in pain. She let go of the baby but it clung to her nipple. The pain was such that Pootana began to change back into the demon she really was—ugly and evil smelling.

Pootana shrieked for mercy but the baby Krishna went on sucking and sucking—until he had sucked all of Pootana's life away.

The Serpent King

KALIYA, THE SERPENT KING was no ordinary snake. He had five heads and was so large that he could crush humans to death in a matter of seconds. The Serpent King lived under the darkest whirlpools of the Yamuna River and this is where he held his court. Whenever he so wished, he would rise out of the water and lay waste the countryside, ferociously breathing fire and black smoke wherever he went.

Krishna was almost twelve years old by now. Even at this tender age he was the acknowledged leader among his friends and looked upon with great respect by the large community of nomadic cowherds that moved wherever the pasture was good.

One day, a group of cowherds came to Krishna and said, 'Kaliya must be stopped. He has already swallowed three hundred chickens, a hundred and seventy-eight goats, and eighty-three cows. Yesterday he killed the black-smith's son. This is the last straw. Anyone that tries to cross the river, swim, graze cattle, grow watermelons, milk goats or even walk by the river is in danger. Something must be done.'

Krishna collected a group of brave friends and walked towards the edge of the water. Suddenly a cloud of black smoke rose above the river, shooting flames swirled upwards and, in one quick swipe, Kaliya encircled all of Krishna's friends in the curl of his body and dragged them down to the bottom of the river.

Having done their dirty deed, the five dreaded heads bobbed up again, breaking the surface of the water. This time the Serpent King was floating along casually, mockingly.

Krishna took one flying leap and landed on all the five hooded heads of the dreaded snake. He crushed one head under one arm and another head under another arm. With his feet he began a heavy-footed dance on the remaining three.

Kaliya felt as if all the mountains of the Himalayas were raining on his head. Such was the power of Krishna's feet.

He decided to dive into his under-water court. He would drown Krishna this way.

Krishna held his breath as Kaliya dived deeper and deeper.

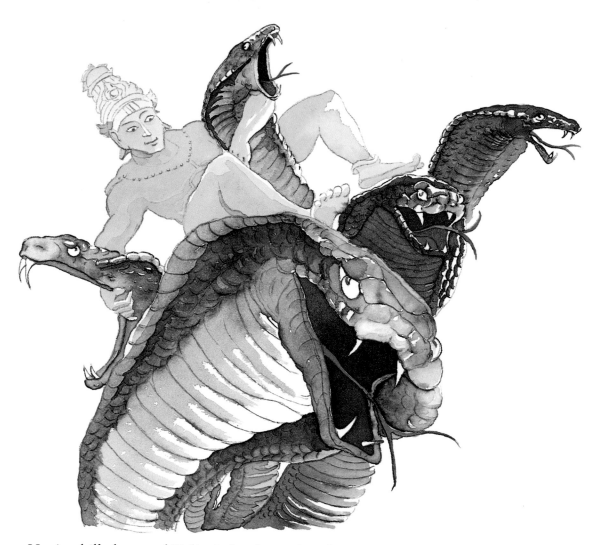

Having killed two of Kaliya's heads Krishna began squeezing the next two under his arms until they also gave up and died.

The last head fought on. It snapped and lunged at Krishna and breathed fire on him, but Krishna trapped that head, too, under his arm and began to squeeze.

Kaliya gave a few last gasps and died.

Krishna swam into Kaliya's court where all his friends, now quite pale and blue, lay dying. He pulled them out of the water and laid them down on the shore. Then, with his mouth, he breathed life into each one saying, 'Dearest friends, it is time to awaken. Kaliya our enemy is dead. Awaken. Awaken. It is time to tend our cows.'

How Krishna Killed the Wicked King Kans

'LET US BEGIN a week of festivities,' the wicked King Kans proclaimed from his throne. 'All our enemies are dead or locked up. This winter's crop has been blessedly plentiful. Our granaries are full of wheat and dried beans and our treasure houses are filled with gold and jewels. We have decided to celebrate with elephant races, wrestling matches, musical plays and banquets. See that all is arranged.'

'Not a bad idea. Not bad at all,' said one of his informers. 'The granaries and treasure houses are full and *most* of your enemies are disposed of.

King Kans turned sharply towards him, 'What do you mean by that remark?'

'Which remark, your highness?'

Kans snarled. 'That *most* of my enemies are disposed of.'

'Well, your highness, that is just what I meant. Your father is in a dungeon and your sister and her husband are in jail. *Most* of them are taken care of.'

'But not all?'

'Well, there is the small matter of Krishna, the cowherd, your sister's son. He is a youth now and very highly regarded across the river. Not everyone realizes that he is your heir. If he decides to spread this information around, your people could . . . could possibly . . . there is a chance . . . that they could reject you . . . in favour . . . of your nephew.'

'Nephew?' thundered Kans. 'I have no nephew.' The words of the wise Sage uttered almost eighteen years ago at his sister's wedding clutched at his heart and gave it a deadly squeeze. The Sage had said, 'Do not let this couple go. Do you not know that you are doomed to die at the hands of their child?'

Kans's heart beat so hard he thought it would burst out of his chest.

'If you are talking about Krishna, then the matter was taken care of years ago by the demon, Pootana. Pootana never fails.'

'She must have failed this time. Krishna not only lives but he is reputed to be both popular and strong.'

'How do you know this?' Kans asked.

'All you have to do is to cross the Yamuna River . . . and you will hear of no one else. The people say Krishna is a god . . . that he killed Kaliya the dreaded Serpent King, that he sucked away the life of a nurse who tried to poison him . . . that. . .'

'Ahhhhh,' cried Kans. He had begun to understand.

'As for his strength,' went on the informer, 'I understand Krishna and his foster-brother Balram are champion wrestlers. Even on this side of the river people are beginning to turn to him for help.'

Another evil scheme had started to form in Kans's mind. 'I know what we must do. Next week, for our festivities, let us put extra emphasis on the wrestling matches. Let us send out a challenge to all the young wrestlers within a thousand miles to come and try to beat our court champions, Chanur and Mustik.' Kans grinned with satisfaction. Chanur and Mustik were giants, stronger than bull buffaloes. They would take care of Krishna, once and for all.

Kans called his drummers and heralds and asked them to travel everywhere within a thousand miles of the palace with an announcement of the King's festivities, most especially the wrestling match.

'Come here,' Kans said, calling his chief herald towards him. 'There is a cowherd by the name of Krishna. I want you to make sure that he not only hears the announcement, but that he and his brother accept the challenge. How you do this, I leave up to you. Here is a ruby for your extra trouble.'

The chief herald pocketed the ruby. He had of course heard of Krishna. Had not everyone? The herald had also seen Chanur and Mustik in action and no wrestlers on earth had been able to defeat them. Poor Krishna did not stand a chance.

The entire kingdom now heard about the festivities.

'Hear ye, hear ye.' the chief herald shouted above the drum rolls. 'Hear ye, hear ye. The almighty, all knowing, all seeing, father of the universe, King of Mathura, King Kans hereby offers a challenge to any youth within a thousand miles of his palace. If he can defeat the wrestlers Chanur and Mustik in a fair match, he will be rewarded with a treasure chest.'

Seeing Krishna and Balram standing with a group of friends, the herald went on, 'The court has heard of these two brothers by reputation. Will they agree to fight like champions or will they sneak away like cowards?'

The taunt had its desired effect.

'I will fight. I will accept the challenge,' Krishna said.

'So will I,' Balram followed.

'Well, then, it is all settled,' the herald said, his lips curling up in triumph. 'We will let the public know. It will be the match of the century.'

Wrestling matches are supposed to be played according to fair rules, but King Kans had no intention of letting Krishna survive.

On the day of the match, he called his Prime Minister aside and told him the plan. 'As soon as Krishna and Balram come into the wrestling ring, let loose the mad, wild elephant we have chained in the barn. Say that the elephant broke away by accident, but make sure that it charges straight at those two young men. They cannot possibly survive. We will all mourn the accident of course, and offer the family gold in compensation. Krishna will be dead and the world will consider us generous beyond measure.'

'What a perfect plan, your highness,' said the Prime Minister.

'There is a back-up plan too, if the first one fails. Chanur and Mustik will be waiting. If the mad elephant does not succeed, our wrestlers will go in and finish the brothers.'

'Perfect. Perfect. Your highness thinks of everything.'

All the spectators were now collected around the wrestling ring, with King Kans seated higher up on a dais.

Krishna and Balram walked into the ring.

The crowd got up on its feet and cheered.

King Kans did not like that too much. 'You won't be cheering for long,' he muttered between his teeth.

Just then a gate flew open and a trumpeting elephant came charging towards the brothers.

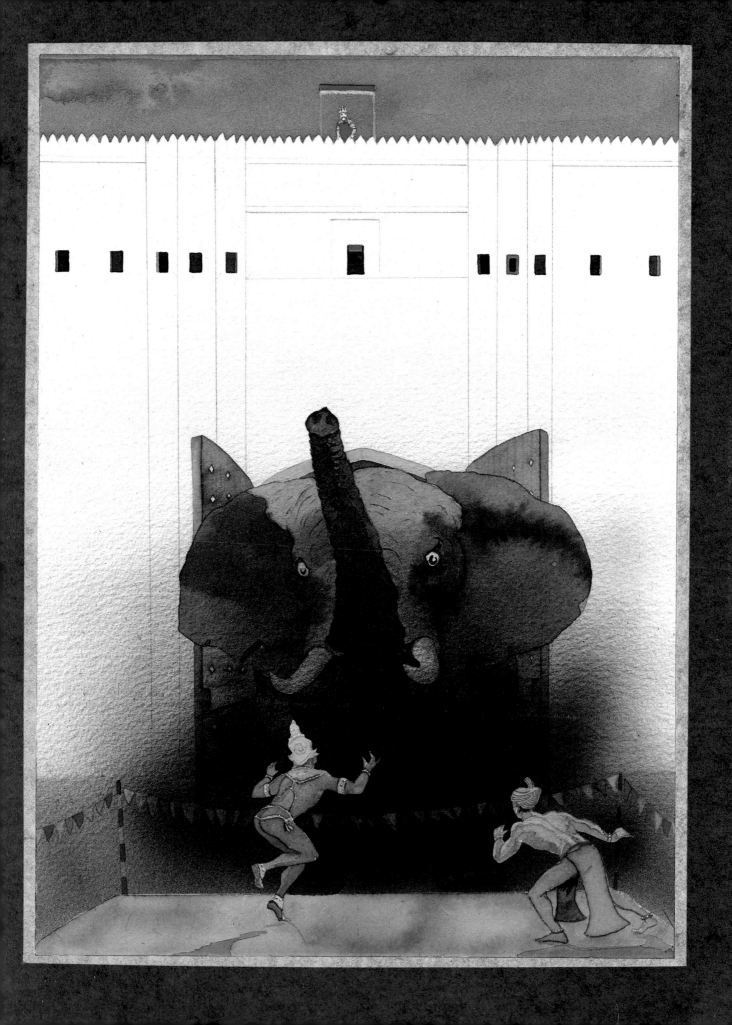

Without a second's hesitation, Krishna leapt upon the elephant's back and with his long, strong arms, squeezed its neck until the creature crumpled under him.

Dead. The elephant was dead.

The crowd got up and cheered.

Kans stared in disbelief. 'Hurry, hurry, send in Chanur and Mustik.'

The two giant wrestlers strutted into the ring, their well-oiled muscles rippling in the sun. They looked more like mammoths than men. Their shoulders were massive.

'I will take Chanur,' said Krishna.

'And I will handle Mustik,' said Balram.

Krishna took a flying leap at Chanur and wrestled him to the ground. Then he twisted his neck and broke it.

Balram picked Mustik up by his right leg and threw him to the ground. Then he squeezed his chest in a bear hug and burst his heart.

Both wrestlers were dead.

The crowd got up on its feet and cheered.

Kans called out to his soldiers, 'Get your swords. Kill those scoundrels. Rush in and kill them.'

But before the soldiers could move, Krishna jumped upon the dais and pulled Kans off the throne.

'You evil man, your time has come. You killed all my sisters and now you will die a terrible death. Krishna picked Kans up with both his arms and hurled him against a wall.

That was the end of Kans.

Krishna freed his parents who were still in jail and his grandfather, who was still locked up in a dungeon.

'Grandfather,' he said, 'the throne is yours. We know you will rule justly.'

'As you will after me,' the grandfather replied, tears rolling down his cheeks. 'The people have, at last, been freed from tyranny.'

TIME FOR THE DEAD

Starting just after the day of the full-moon in early September and continuing through the next two weeks, my family liked to remember all our relatives who had died. On my grandfather's Moon-Day, year after year, we prayed, fed our priests and ate mightily well ourselves. We thought of our grandfather and hoped that he might be thinking of us. My grandfather was the first man—the first human being—that I had watched dying. I had not actually seen him die. I remember with great guilt now that when a cousin came running to inform me that my grandfather was actually dead, I felt cheated. Cheated because I had missed the moment. I had not seen human life stop. He had been dying for months, you see. I had watched his six-foot tall frame shrink while the skin around his bones became almost translucent. His arrogance kept him going. His arrogance and his brilliance. He was just too powerful to be sucked away. So he went on living, much longer than he probably should have.

I remember one still May evening. It was too hot to sleep indoors so cots with crisp white sheets had been laid out on the lawn. There must have been at least forty cots. We were a large family, what with cousins, aunts and uncles. All of us were uneasy because of Grandfather's condition. An oxygen tent had been placed near his cot and all the elders were taking turns holding the oxygen mask to his face. Once, when it was my mother's turn, she turned to me and said in a whisper, 'Hold the mask. I have to go inside for a minute.'

I felt like a soldier that had been called to duty. I held the mask up to my grandfather's mouth and nose without blinking or moving a muscle.

There must have been something about the position of my rigid hand that my grandfather did not care for. He lifted his very frail arm with great effort and gave my hand a gentle push.

In that one touch—that last touch—were all the moments I had shared with my grandfather. There was the time when I was five and he had dipped his finger into his glass of whisky-soda to give me my first lick of alcohol. There was the time when he had lifted me up to ride with him in his phaeton carriage. And there was the time when he was teaching me chess. He had put his hand on mine and helped me lift my Queen into the air. 'Now knock the King down and say "checkmate". You have won. Don't you see, you have won.'

Doda
and
Dodi

DODA AND DODI were a brother and sister who loved each other very much. It so happened that Doda, together with his wife and children, was very rich and that Dodi, along with her husband and children, was very poor.

As September approached, Doda went to his wife and said, 'Oh, mother-of-my-children, I have decided to go to the holy city of Gaya on the tenth day of the moon as that is the moon day of my father's death. I will feed the priests and pray there. I want you to be very generous here. Offer prayers, invite lots of priests and all the family and feed them with an open heart. Oh yes, by the way, please do not ignore my sister. She is . . . not so well off . . . so keep a watchful eye over her. She needs all the assistance we can give her. And when she and her family come here for my father's Moon Day feast, make sure that they are well fed. In fact, give them lots of food to take home as well. They will not ask for it, knowing them, but I know that it would help their family a lot. Be nice to Dodi or I will be very upset.'

Saying this, the brother left a large bag of gold coins for his wife to use and set off for Gaya.

Doda's wife happened to be a rather unpleasant person. She sat down and wrote out an invitation for Dodi. This is what she wrote:

> In memory of your father
> You and your family are cordially invited
> Next Thursday
> To attend his Moon Day festivities
> Come only if all the roots shake
> Do not come at all if the leaves shake.

Doda's wife folded the note and handed it to a servant, saying, 'Go and take this to Dodi's hut and deliver it safely into her hands.'

Dodi did, indeed, live in a hut. It was small, but neat and clean, with every brass pot gleaming from years of painstaking scrubbing.

Dodi saw the servant from her brother's house coming towards her hut. 'Oh,' she thought, 'he must have the invitation for my father's Moon Day festivities.' She was so looking forward to going over. She had loved her father with the same devotion that she had for her brother. She would go early in the morning and help her sister-in-law grind the split peas and make the mounds of dough that would be needed for all the stuffed breads.

But when Dodi read her sister-in-law's invitation, she was taken aback. 'What on earth could she mean?' Dodi said aloud. 'What a strange invitation. Whatever she had in mind, only she knows. I'm going to go anyway.'

As soon as the first rays of the sun touched her hut, Dodi set out for her brother's house, and there she slaved all morning in the kitchen. She moved the huge grinding stone back and forth until her arms ached. She must have rolled out and fried at least a thousand breads. Then, when the priests had to be fed while they sat in neat rows on the ground, she served them, with her back bent for hours at a time. When it was time for the family to eat, Dodi's sister-in-law fed her own children but refused to offer even a morsel to Dodi or her family.

Dodi did not want to ask. No food was offered so she and her family just went hungry.

It was all very well for her husband and herself. They could bear it, but their children began to whimper and cry, 'We are hungry, we are hungry.'

Now, since Dodi had been rolling out the breads, her hands were all sticky with dough. She called to her children, 'I'm about to wash my hands of all the dough that is sticking to them. You catch the water as it comes out of the drain and drink it.'

What else could Dodi do? This is all she could offer her children.

Since she and her family were quite worn out, they all fell asleep on the floor.

In the middle of the night Dodi sat bolt upright. She was wide, wide awake and just so very hungry. Her sister-in-law's household was still filled with all the lovely aromas of all the good foods that had been cooked and eaten that day. Dodi found herself walking towards the kitchen in the dark. There, in a covered container, with the moonlight gleaming on it, was a stack of delicious breads. Just one of them would satisfy her hunger and that of her family. She opened the container, stretched out her hand and stopped.

Her sister-in-law did not want her to eat those breads. It would be stealing. But nobody was watching. Perhaps she could take one for her family. Just then, she looked out of the window. How wrong of her to think that no one was watching. The Moon God was watching—silent as ever.

She could not do it. She closed the bread container and went back to her sleeping family. She shook them awake, 'Come on, get up, get up, let us go home. It is time to go home.'

'We are so hungry,' cried her children.

'I will get you some food when we are home,' Dodi said to them.

But there was no food at home, either.

'We are hungry,' said the children. 'Please feed us.'

'Soon, soon,' answered Dodi.

'How can you feed us soon?' asked the children, 'We have not seen you cooking anything.'

'I am just about to start,' said Dodi.

Saying this, Dodi put a few stones in a brass pot, covered it up, and set it on the stove.

The family were so weak and weary that they fell asleep again.

Again, Dodi woke up with a start. She had been dreaming that her house was filled with the delicious aroma of rice pudding. She was about to shut her eyes again when the children started crying, 'We smell rice pudding. We are hungry. We are hungry.'

Dodi felt she had better go to the pot on the stove and shake it around. That might console the children. But when she went to the pot she found a fire under it, and steam coming out from the top.

Inside there was indeed rice pudding.

It was her father who was responsible. He had been watching from heaven and had seen how hard his daughter had worked that day. He had decided to lend a hand. Not only was there rice pudding in the pot, but breads and vegetables and split peas, arranged around the kitchen all cooked and ready. The hut had been transformed into a stately mansion. There were pouches everywhere filled with gold coins and jewellery. There were cases of gold necklaces, bracelets, ear-rings, nose-rings and toe-rings.

Dodi was delighted. She fed her family, cleaned up the pots, and then settled down for a well-deserved rest.

Meanwhile, something very strange was happening in Gaya. When Doda stooped to offer water to the priests, he found that he was pouring out blood.

The priests moved back, saying, 'What kind of charity is this? You come to offer us food and water, and then give us blood!'

Doda stopped short, horrified. It did not take him long to understand.

Something was wrong at home. It must be his wife, who he knew was often unkind to Dodi. His wife had probably mistreated her.

The brother immediately began his journey back home. Meanwhile, Dodi, now comfortably rich, decided to invite her sister-in-law to dinner. So she wrote out a note saying:

In memory of my father
I would like to invite you and your children
To dinner
Tomorrow.

She sent off her eldest son with the note.

When Dodi's sister-in-law received it, she laughed.

'So, she is going to entertain in her hut, is she? I shall make a laughing-stock of her.'

Just before she went to the dinner, she picked up a clay pot from her kitchen and took it to her barn. There, she filled it with cow dung and then tied a

leaf around the top to close it up. She was going to offer the clay pot as a present to Dodi. What could be more appropriate to the setting?

She laughed long and loud to herself. Then she tucked the pot in the crook of her left arm and set off for Dodi's hut.

There was no hut to be seen, only a large mansion. It was much larger than her own, Dodi's sister-in-law noticed with much dissatisfaction.

When she went in, her face turned even more sour as she saw an army of uniformed servants and her sister-in-law's family decked out in brocades and jewels.

She sat down to eat, along with the other hundreds of guests, her clay pot still tucked in the crook of her arm. Seeing Dodi's new circumstances, she thought it would be *she* who would be the laughing-stock if the guests ever found out that her present was cow dung.

So she held onto her pot.

But not for long.

Dodi approached her and said, 'Dear sister-in-law, I noticed that you have been carrying a clay pot all this time. Let me relieve you of it.'

'Oh, no, it's quite all right.'

'I'm sure you brought it for us. What is it?'

'Ohh . . . nothing . . . I mean . . . it is just . . . yoghurt,' the sister-in-law lied.

'Well, if it's yoghurt, I will serve it to you and all our guests.'

So saying, Dodi took the clay pot from her sister-in-law and began serving from it. To the sister-in-law's surprise—and great relief—what came out of the pot was—yoghurt!

You see, Dodi's father was still watching from heaven. However unkind his daughter-in-law was, she was his son's wife and his grandchildren's mother. He did not want the family to be embarrassed.

Dodi's sister-in-law did not return home happy. She felt that all the guests there were probably comparing Dodi's festivities and food with her own and that her own had not been half as good.

So she decided to plan another dinner—much more lavish than Dodi's—and to invite all the same guests.

This time she even served Dodi and her family. While Dodi and her husband ate, their children refused all food. Instead, they began to sing:

> 'You did not feed me when I was poor and starving
> You only invited me here
> Because now I have fine feathers
> So
> Instead of feeding me
> Feed my ear-ring
> Feed my nose-ring
> Feed my toe-ring
> And feed my fine feathers all.'

After their song, they got up, took their parents' hands, and left.

Soon afterwards Doda returned from his trip to Gaya. He was very angry with his wife for mistreating Dodi, but his wife answered, 'Oh father-of-my-children, how can you be so cruel to me? I have been *so* good to Dodi. In fact, Dodi was *just* here for dinner.'

'Did you feed her?'

'Of course. I fed her *so* generously. How could you talk to me this way . . . when . . . when . . . I'm not even well.'

And Doda's wife took herself to bed, where she stayed, pretending to be ill.

Some days later, she called Doda to her bedside and said, 'Oh father-of-my-children, I feel so unwell. Could you please do something for me? I have filled two pots with delicious things. The smaller one is for my mother. Could you take it to her home? I have prepared a nice, large pot for you to take to your sister's house. You can deliver both on your way to work.'

'Whatever you say, mother-of-my-children,' Doda replied. 'I shall do it today.'

'One other thing,' added his wife. 'This is a special request for Dodi. Her present is a surprise. Tell her that if she really wants to enjoy it, then she should open it behind seven locked doors. She should hire singers and musicians to sit outside. Whatever sounds come from inside the locked room, the musicians should try to imitate them. It will really be a lot of fun.'

'Whatever you say, mother-of-my-children,' said Doda.

On his way to work, Doda, suspecting his wife was up to no good, switched the pots. He left the large pot with his wife's mother—with all his wife's instructions about the locked doors and the musicians—and took the small pot to his sister.

He stayed with his sister as she opened her gift. The pot was filled with delicious sweets. The brother was relieved and the sister pleased that there was harmony in the household again. Meanwhile, Doda's mother-in-law had collected all the singers and musicians and put herself behind seven locked doors.

With great glee, she opened her pot, wondering just what wonderful gifts her rich daughter had sent her.

But out of the pot came scorpions and snakes and angry little bees. They began attacking the old woman. She tried to run out, but all the doors were locked. 'Oh, I'm stung,' she yelled. The musicians, asked to copy all the sounds coming out from the locked room, sang, 'Do, re, mi, I'm stung, I'm stung.'

The old woman yelled, 'Help, I'm bitten, I'm bitten.'

The musicians sang, 'Do, re, mi, I'm bitten, I'm bitten.'

The old woman cried, 'Someone help, I'm being killed.'

The musicians sang, 'Do, re, mi, I'm being killed, I'm being killed.'

Now the old woman's family was listening outside. They got increasingly worried at the strange nature of the sounds and began unlocking the doors.

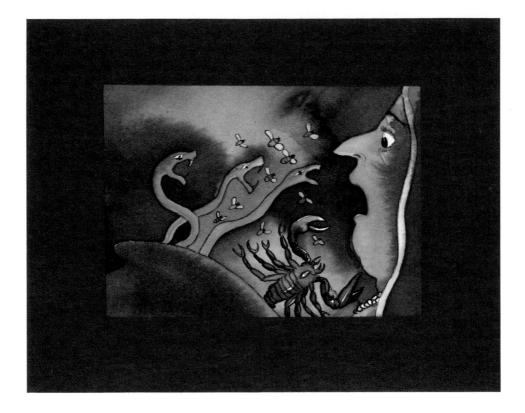

Inside they found the old woman, swollen with bites and stings, but quite alive.

They helped her out and treated her with lotions and potions.

Meanwhile, back at Doda's house, lotions and potions were doing his wife no good.

When Doda returned home, his wife was still in bed.

'Did you deliver the pots?' she asked.

Yes, mother-of-my-children. Just as you said,' answered Doda. 'But what is the matter with you? You do not seem to get better. We have called all the best doctors, and they cannot find anything wrong with you.'

'What do these doctors know. I cannot eat at all, as you can see. I have completely lost my appetite. See how my bones creak?' She moved her body and, indeed, all Doda could hear was crackle, crackle, crunch.

Next day, as Doda was leaving for work his good neighbours called out, 'Kindly step in here for a moment. We have something to show you. Instead of going to work today, just stay here and watch your wife's antics.'

Doda watched from their window.

He watched his wife get out of bed and go to the kitchen to feed herself mounds of sweets and halvas and puddings. Then she went into her garden, pulled up some sugar cane, and chewed on that for a while. Then she went back to the kitchen and fried up a batch of breads and crisp wafers. She ate the breads. Then, when it was time for her husband to return, she did something very odd with the wafers. Before getting back into bed to wait for her husband, she tied them to her body under her clothing.

So, thought Doda. It was the wafers that crackled and crunched. His wife was *so* clever.

When he got home, she pretended to be iller than ever.

Doda, playing her game, said, 'Dear mother-of-my-children, you look so ill and your bones are crackling more than ever. We have tried all the doctors. Tell me, tell me, is there any cure left? I will do anything you ask. I just want you to be well again.'

'Dearest father-of-my-children,' his wife answered, 'mine is a hopeless case. I have seen all the doctors and tried all their remedies. All that is left for me is death.' But then she went on. 'However, a fortuneteller did visit me today. And he suggested something that he said was a sure cure.'

'Today?' asked Doda. He had watched her all day and she had been alone.

'Yes,' she sighed, 'He came today. I'm really not sure I can tell you his cure. It is not very pleasant.'

'However unpleasant,' said Doda, 'I will see it is done. All I want is for you to be well again.'

'Since you ask,' said his wife. 'Well, this fortuneteller said that the only way my life can be saved is if Dodi, her husband and children, shave their heads, blacken their faces, sit backwards on asses, and come here beating broken clay pots, singing, "Long live Doda's wife, long live Doda's wife".'

'This is easy,' said Doda. 'I am sure my sister would not object to it. Not if it will save your life. After all, what is hair? It is like grass in the monsoon season. It will grow again quickly. And as for blackened faces, they can be washed off easily. Do not worry your sweet head in the least. I will arrange it immediately. All I want is for you to be well and for this household to flourish.'

His wife tried hard not to smile. She was finally going to humiliate Dodi.

Doda, instead of going to his sister, went directly to his mother-in-law. Just before he entered her house, he adjusted his expression. He put on a long, unhappy face and had tears in his eyes.

All the children and grandchildren in his mother-in-law's household began calling, 'Uncle is here, Uncle is here.'

The mother-in-law was not too sure how she felt about him. The last time he had visited, he had left a large clay pot filled with vicious creatures. What did he want this time, she wondered?

His very sad expression worried her. Was something wrong?

'Is everything all right with you?'

'Oh, I am fine,' he answered, 'but your daughter is *very* sick. In fact, she is on her deathbed.'

'Oh, heavens,' said his mother-in-law. 'Is there anything we can do to help?'

'Well,' said Doda, 'a fortuneteller came to see her today. . .'

'Yes?' prompted his mother-in-law.

'I hesitate to ask. It is not pleasant,' said Doda.

'Do ask,' said his mother-in-law. 'There is nothing I would not do for my daughter.'

'Well,' said Doda, 'it involves your whole family. Your sons, daughters-in-law and children.'

'We will all willingly do whatever is necessary.'

'What the fortuneteller said was that the only remedy was for you and your entire family to shave their heads, blacken their faces, sit backwards on asses and come to our house beating on broken clay pots, singing, "Stupid daughter, stupid daughter." It may seem odd, but that is what the fortuneteller said.'

'It certainly is odd,' said the mother-in-law, 'but if this will save my daughter's life, I will do it.'

So the mother-in-law sent one son to hire asses, another to get the barber, and yet another to grind some coal.

The entire family had their heads shaved. Then they blackened their faces with ground coal, sat backwards on the asses, and started towards the house of Doda's wife beating on broken clay pieces and singing, 'Stupid daughter, stupid daughter.'

Doda's wife, meanwhile, was awaiting, with much glee, a procession led by Dodi.

She put on her prettiest sari and took a position on her balcony. She could see quite a distance from there.

A procession was approaching.

Doda's wife almost danced with excitement.

'This must be good for you,' said Doda. 'You already look much better.'

As the procession neared the house, Doda's wife sang gleefully to her husband:

'The tricks of women are so bold.
They can sit at home and shake the world.'

To which Doda sang back:

'Men too, know a few things, you see.
Is that Dodi, or is that your mummy?'

Doda's wife now saw that it was her mother who was leading the procession. She almost died of shame.

Her mother came up to her and said, 'Well, daughter, you seem fine to me. Why did you ask us to humiliate ourselves like this?'

At this point, Doda's wife burst into tears and told her whole story. 'I have been so wicked,' she cried, 'and I have been punished. From now on, I will be a good wife to Doda, a good sister-in-law to Dodi, and a good daughter to my dear, departed father-in-law.'

DUSSEHRA,
THE FESTIVAL OF VICTORY

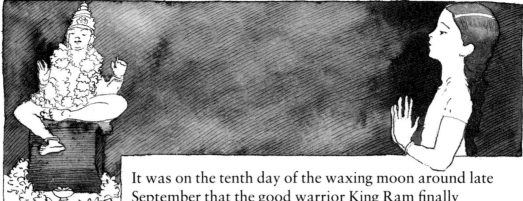

It was on the tenth day of the waxing moon around late September that the good warrior King Ram finally defeated Ravan, the evil demon with ten heads, in a long and deadly battle that took place in a country we now call Sri Lanka. All this happened thousands of years ago but even today the story is acted out in every city and village of India. It is a nationwide celebration of Good over Evil.

In our family, we children would make crude, clay statues of the demon, Ravan, and then lay them down on our driveway. Shouting, 'Kill, kill, kill,' we would hop onto our bicycles and ride all over the statues, crushing them to pieces. Tame stuff, I know. The problem was that our family was never a family of warriors. The only wars we waged were with pens and pencils. Even fifteen hundred years ago, my ancestors made their living writing, not fighting.

Because, at this festival, every family worships the 'weapons of its trade,' my mother would first set up a statue of the good King Ram in our prayer room, properly garlanded with a fresh marigold necklace.

Under the statue where some people arranged guns and swords, my mother arranged, very neatly, some of the oddest things—my father's Parker pen, my school pencil, paintbrushes, nibs, rulers, even bottles of royal blue Quink. All these things needed to be blessed and Dussehra was the best time for it.

This suited me perfectly. I do not know if the good King Ram was aware of it, but by the age of six, I had already developed a raging passion for stationery. I loved the feel of thick, smooth paper and the smell of freshly sharpened pencils. In a drawer marked 'Private', I had put together a collection that boasted a single pencil that would write in five colours, a fat red fountain pen with a black tassel, and a sable-hair brush that was fine enough to paint the veins of leaves.

It was heartwarming to know that someone in heaven was interested in my collection. If the good King Ram would bless my pens and pencils, I would willingly bicycle over the demon Ravan for him as many times as he pleased.

How Ram
Defeated the
Demon King Ravan

I King Dashrat's Special Heir

LONG, LONG AGO there lived in the northern kingdom of Kosala, a warrior king named Dashrat. His capital city was Ayodhya. And what a city it was! It sprawled on the banks of the Saryu River, with elegant seven-storey mansions rising gracefully from formal parks and gardens. Its granaries were filled with wheat, its treasure houses with gold. Young people here dressed with such style and imagination, buying their woollens and colourful silks from caravans that criss-crossed the globe.

Elephants with tinkling bells tied to their feet and warriors brave as lions defended the city. There was no war for the elephants and warriors to go to, though, for the kingdom of Kosala was at peace.

King Dashrat, living in a snow-white palace on top of a hill, ruled honourably, wisely and with strength. His people were happy and contented and his enemies too afraid to challenge him.

The only man in Kosala who was not entirely satisfied with his life was King Dashrat himself. He was very, very old, and had no heirs to inherit his throne. He had three wives but no child to carry on his good work for the people of his kingdom.

Dashrat begged his priest for help.

'There must be a way,' he cried. 'Let us offer prayers in front of a big sacrificial fire. Perhaps the gods will hear us.'

A huge fire was made and butter dribbled into it.

'Oh gods, hear us,' prayed the priest.

And the gods listened.

Gods have their own reasons for the things they do. Their reason this time was Ravan.

Ravan was a demon king, dark as a thundercloud and as wicked as Dashrat was good. If Dashrat ruled over the kingdom of Kosala in the north, Ravan ruled the Island of Demons, Lanka, far away in the south. If Dashrat's capital city was almost as fair as heaven, Ravan's was designed by the architect of heaven. If Dashrat had one head and two arms, like most men, Ravan had ten heads and twenty arms. Ravan could smile a ten-mouthed smile, twirl ten moustaches at once, and let loose a rainfall of arrows from ten golden bows.

But that is not what troubled the gods. In a moment of weakness, the gods

had granted Ravan a wish. Ravan, shrewd as he was, had asked the gods to arrange it so that no god in heaven and no creature from the underworld would be able to kill him. Ravan wanted to be immortal. The gods had unfortunately agreed.

The result was that Ravan and his fellow demons flew around heaven and earth drinking blood, eating people and changing shape at will to get at their victims. Ravan and his demons had become so powerful and so wicked that they could, at times, even stop the smoke given off by holy fires from reaching heaven, and this angered the gods.

While King Dashrat was preparing his sacrifice on earth, a god in heaven was saying, 'There has got to be a way to stop Ravan. If we cannot stop him, who can? We are supposed to be gods.'

Another god said, 'Whoever granted that wish to Ravan was *so* stupid . . . so very stupid.'

A third god said, 'Let us not fight amongst ourselves but plan ahead. The wish we granted actually stops gods from heaven and the underworld from destroying Ravan. It says nothing about men and animals who live on earth. . .'

'That is true,' said a fourth god. 'But Ravan is so strong that it would take a very special man.'

'I could assist this . . . very special man . . . by being born again in his body,' said a fifth god, who happened to be Vishnu, the Preserver of Life.

Just then, smoke from King Dashrat's sacrifice managed, somehow, to reach heaven.

The gods had found a way. They would give King Dashrat an heir. A very special heir.

On earth a black giant dressed in crimson appeared in King Dashrat's fire. His dark, silky hair fluttered in the breeze like a flag in the wind. Handing Dashrat a bowl filled with rice pudding, he intoned, 'Come, divide this amongst your wives. They will give you the sons you desire.' Then the giant disappeared in the smoke.

Dashrat took the bowl to his first wife, Kaushalya, and gave her half of the pudding. Out of what was left, he gave half to his second wife Sumitra. Out of what remained, he gave half to his third wife Kaikeyi. A little bit of pudding was still in the bowl. He gave that to Sumitra, saying, 'Here, finish it up.'

Kaushalya duly gave birth to a son, Ram. Kaikeyi was next, with a son named Bharat. Sumitra was last. She had been given two helpings, so she had twin boys, Laxshman and Shatrughan.

As the boys grew older, Laxshman grew very attached to his eldest brother, Ram, and Shatrughan to his brother Bharat. All the brothers, however, were very close and loved each other.

It was Ram, of course, strong, handsome Ram, who was heir to the throne and in whose body there lived, very quietly, the soul of a god.

When the boys were sixteen a wise Sage and family adviser said, 'It is time

Ram and Laxshman were taught how to fight demons. I will take the boys away and begin their instruction.'

Ram was taught sacred verses that would increase his strength a hundred times, and he was shown how to use magical weapons that came straight from heaven. Both boys perfected their archery and their use of deadly flying discs.

On their way home, following this instruction, the threesome passed through the lands of the good King Janak. A wedding party was being held in the capital city and it was a very special wedding party.

Janak's daughter, Sita, was about to pick a husband from all the men who were assembled there. Just one condition had been attached to the men's chances of happiness. They had, first of all, to bend and string a very heavy bow.

Almost every prince, king and nobleman present wanted to marry Sita because she was, quite simply, the most beautiful girl on earth. Her skin was soft and golden, her eyes large and shining, her lips red and full and her lustrous black hair so long that it reached her ankles. As Sita walked the belts draped around her hips jingled gently and her airy, silver scarves swayed in the breeze. When Sita smiled, she was as dazzling as the sun. Sita was quite irresistible.

One man after another had tried to lift the bow, but it could not be lifted, let alone bent and strung. It weighed as much as a mountain. King Janak despaired of ever marrying off his daughter, when Ram appeared on the scene.

Sita was watching from a window and fell instantly in love with the handsome prince. 'Oh,' she prayed, 'please let him bend the bow.'

Ram looked down at the bow and said to himself, 'No human can lift this. It is god Shiva's bow from heaven.' But when he bent down, he found that he could lift it with ease. He pressed one end under his foot and bent the other enough to string it. He bent is so much that, much to the amazement of all who were present, the bow snapped in two.

Ram and Sita were wed in front of a fire. Sita's father showered the bride and groom with gifts of elephants, horses, dogs, and baskets filled with gold beads and turquoise to take back to Ayodhya.

The young couple settled down to live together in a shining palace of black stone. Wherever they walked, their love for each other made flowers bloom and leaves brighten in colour.

But trouble was brewing in King Dashrat's snow-white palace on top of the hill.

II Ram is Banished

KING DASHRAT had been doing some serious thinking. He was getting too old. It was time he handed over the throne to his son Ram. 'Why wait to die?' he thought. 'It would give me so much pleasure to see my dear son Ram sit on my throne and rule.'

He made an announcement in court, 'Let the preparations for my son's coronation begin.'

Meanwhile, Queen Kaikeyi, Bharat's mother, was idle.

She had a scheming, hunchback maid who came to her and said, 'Today you are lolling happily on pillows, sucking a mango, but your tomorrows are bound to be miserable.'

'What on earth can you mean?' Kaikeyi asked.

'When Ram is king, no one will care for you or for your dear son, Bharat.'

'What nonsense you talk,' Kaikeyi said, delicately wiping mango juice off her fingers. 'I love Ram and he *is* the heir.'

'Not if you change things.'

'But how can I?'

'Easily,' said the scheming maid. 'Remember, a very long time ago, you saved Dashrat's life during a war, and he said he would grant you any two wishes.'

'Yes, and I said I would ask for my wishes later, when I knew what I wanted,' said Kaikeyi, sucking out some more juice from her mango.

'Exactly. Ask for them now. Ask for Bharat to be crowned king and for Ram to be banished to the forest for fourteen years.'

Now, King Dashrat's palace had a room where anyone could go if they were feeling angry or upset.

Kaikeyi went into the Anger Room and threw herself on the floor.

Soon King Dashrat came in to find out what was troubling her. Kaikeyi was so very pretty. The King could never ignore her for long.

'What is the matter, my sweet wife?' King Dashrat asked.

'Oh, nothing very much,' Queen Kaikeyi answered.

'It cannot be nothing or you would not be in this room. Besides, your eyes are all puffy. Tell me sweet, what is the matter?'

'I want to ask you for my two wishes,' Kaikeyi said.

'My Queen, I cannot break my promise to you, you know that. Ask for what you desire,' Dashrat said.

'Crown Bharat king and banish Ram to the forest for fourteen years.'

King Dashrat was stunned into silence. He had *never* broken his word, to god, man or beast. What could he do now? His happiness and his future had all been stolen from him.

'Go and get Ram,' he whispered with difficulty to his servants.

When Ram arrived, his father was far too unhappy to speak. It was Kaikeyi who said, 'Bharat is to be king and you are to be banished for fourteen years.'

'Is this what my dear father desires?' Ram asked.

'Your father is keeping his two promises to me,' Kaikeyi said.

'Then I have no choice, I must honour my father's word. If promises are made, they must be kept. Let Bharat rule. There is not much difference between us. I will leave tomorrow.'

As Ram was preparing to leave, his wife Sita and his brother Laxshman announced that they would accompany him.

'I cannot live without you,' Sita said.

'And I will guard you both,' Laxshman insisted.

'The forest is full of unknown dangers,' Ram said. 'There are only leaves and twigs to sleep on and roots and berries for food. Enjoy the comforts of the palace. Fourteen years will pass quickly.'

But Sita and Laxshman would not be persuaded. The three packed a few belongings and set out for the forest that lay to the south of Kosala.

All of Ayodhya wept at the disaster that had struck them. The birds stopped singing and flowers refused to bloom. As for the King, he fell into a deep gloom. 'I cannot bear it, I cannot bear it,' he cried. One day, his heart broke and he died.

Bharat was sent for. He had to be crowned king, but when he found out what his mother had done, he began to curse her.

He decided to rush to the forest and bring his brother, Ram, back.

Bharat followed after Ram and found him on a quiet mountain top that was covered with spring flowers.

'Our father is dead. Please come back and be king,' Bharat begged.

'I must keep my father's promise,' Ram said. 'If we give in, a little bit here, a little bit there, soon, there will be no honour left. No, I cannot return for fourteen years. I am sure you will rule wisely.'

'I will never wear the crown and never sit on the throne,' Bharat said with great passion. 'Give me your sandals. I will place them on the throne in your name. I will go back to our kingdom only as your caretaker and sit at the foot of the throne. Our family and the people of Kosala will wait patiently for fourteen years until you return. For fourteen years there will be no merriment and no music.'

III The Kidnapping of Sita

AS THE YEARS WORE ON, Ram, Sita and Laxshman walked deeper and deeper into the forest, farther and farther south. Ram was always barefoot. His sandals rested on a throne far away.

Thirteen years passed. The banished Ram and his loving companions were now in the heart of the dreaded Dandaka Forest.

No leaves moved here. The air was as still as death. Scorching fumes rose from large rocks. Life-giving water had deserted the ponds and their bottoms were cracked and hard.

Even though the exiles from Ayodhya were not in Ravan's Lanka, they were close enough to it to feel its wicked influence. Dandaka Forest was controlled by wild demons who drank human blood. The demons were Ravan's people.

'Do not worry,' Ram said to Sita, 'as long as you are with us, we will protect you.'

Just as Ram was saying this, a large demon came flying in from the sky and landed in front of them.

This demon was Ravan's sister, uglier than the worst toad.

Her face was yellow and pitted. Her fingers ended in long, vicious claws. She was as misshapen as a knot on a tree.

She took one look at the handsome Ram and fell head over heels in love with him.

'I want you,' she said to him, her red eyes bulging.

When Ram looked wary, she went on, 'Oh, not to eat. I want to marry you and carry you off to the beautiful kingdom of Lanka.' She thought she was doing Ram a great favour.

'Dear lady, I happen to be happily married already.' He winked at his brother. 'Perhaps this handsome youth here. . .'

'It is you I want and you I will have,' Ravan's sister screamed out as she jumped towards Sita with her evil claws stretched out. But Laxshman was too quick for her. He raised his long knife skywards and brought it down in such a way that it cut off her ears.

Yelling at the top of her voice, the demon ran away into the depths of the forest.

She went to the man Ravan had appointed General of Dandaka Forest.

'Help me, help me, General,' she cried. 'A wretched human has insulted the great Ravan's sister.'

The General immediately took his huge army of demons and swooped down on Ram, Sita and Laxshman. 'Hide in that cave,' Ram told Sita. 'We will take care of this.'

Within seconds, the General was dead and the demon army defeated.

The misshapen demon flew straight to her brother in Lanka crying, 'You must do something. The great Ravan's sister has been insulted, your General

is dead and your army in Dandaka Forest defeated.'

'How did this happen?' the ten-headed demon asked, all his twenty eyes glaring at his sister.

'Humans are the cause of it,' she said, and began to tell her story. When she touched upon the subject of Sita, Ravan became more interested.

'So,' he said, 'what does this Sita look like?'

'Oh, she is beautiful. Much more beautiful, in fact, than any of your wives. She has soft, golden skin and large eyes, very long hair and a tiny, tiny waist . . . she is like a flower in its first bloom.'

Ravan decided that he wanted Sita. 'This situation demands immediate action,' he said. 'Ram needs to be punished and the best way to punish him is to take Sita from him.'

Ravan planned to get help from his clever demon uncle.

'I want to arrange a kidnapping with you,' he announced to his uncle. 'If you could assume the form of a golden deer, you would be able to lure Ram away. I will take care of his brother, Laxshman, *and* his wife Sita,' he added, with a smirk on all of his faces.

Moments later a golden deer with a blue face and a pink belly appeared in the forest.

'What a beautiful creature!' exclaimed Sita. 'Could you catch it for me?'

'I will be back in a moment,' said Ram. 'Stay close to Laxshman and no harm will come to you.'

The deer leapt farther and farther away as Ram kept chasing it. 'This is surely not a deer at all, but a disguised demon,' Ram thought and shot it through its heart with an arrow.

The demon let out a loud, human cry of pain as it died.

Sita heard the cry. 'That was the cry of a human in pain. It must be Ram. Please, Laxshman, go at once. My husband needs you.'

'I cannot leave you,' Laxshman replied.

'You will let your brother die in pain then?' Sita asked.

Laxshman could not bear that thought. He ran off in search of Ram, telling Sita to stay inside the house he had built, where she would be safe.

Ravan was watching all this. His moment had come. He appeared in the form of a hermit.

'Give a poor hermit some food,' he begged outside the house.

Sita's kindly heart made her say, 'I shall come outside in a moment.'

The minute she stepped outside, Ravan fell upon her and carried her off to his chariot of the skies.

Ravan's chariot was as large as a city with hills and ponds and pools and crystal palaces enclosed by an ornate balcony. It was gold coloured and covered with lights of rainbow colours. It was drawn by a team of a thousand horses, though it could fly through the skies without them as well.

With Sita on board, Ravan's chariot began speeding south towards Lanka.

IV The Search for Sita

THERE HAD BEEN BUT ONE OBSERVER of the whole tragedy. An old vulture king, who was sitting quietly in a tree. 'I am old and weak,' he thought, 'but I cannot sit by and watch this wicked deed.'

He flew up from his perch. 'I am King of the Air,' said the Vulture King to Ravan. Do not harm a single hair of this good woman or I will attack.'

'Why don't you go back to sleep? It suits you better,' Ravan answered.

The Vulture King did not have energy to waste on speech. He swooped down on Ravan's chariot, hacking away with his beak and claws at its balconies, at Ravan's head, and at Ravan's horses.

Blood dripped down Ravan's face but the great demon drew out his sword and with one swipe cut off the wings of the Vulture King.

The Vulture King fell dying to the ground.

Ravan's chariot of the skies continued with great speed towards the south. Sita, her hair streaming in the wind, managed, somehow, to slip off her jewellery and let it drop down to earth. Perhaps Ram would find it and see the direction in which the demon was taking her.

Sita's jewellery fell, down, down, down, into the Kingdom of Monkeys and Bears where it was spotted by Hanuman and Sugreev, two monkeys who were sitting on a hill.

'It's raining jewels today,' said Hanuman.

'With my bad luck, I'm surprised it's not rocks,' said Sugreev.

'Want a banana?' asked Hanuman.

'Leave me alone,' said Sugreev, 'I'm depressed. My evil brother, the Monkey King, has thrown me out of the palace. I think I want to die, or go to sleep at least.'

Back in the forest Ram and Laxshman, realizing at once that they had been tricked, ran back towards their house. On their way they passed the dying Vulture King.

'He has ... kidnapped her ... taken her ... south,' the Vulture King managed to say with his final breath, 'Ravan has kidnapped Sita.'

Ram and Laxshman headed south.

'I cannot live without my Sita,' said Ram in deep sorrow.

'We will find her,' his brother Laxshman encouraged.

Soon they came across Hanuman and Sugreev, the two monkeys sitting on a hilltop.

'Have you seen a demon carrying off the fairest woman on this earth?' Laxshman asked.

'Are these her jewels?' Hanuman wanted to know.

'Oh heaven,' said Ram, 'when Sita cries out in pain, who will be there to help her?'

'I have an idea,' said the monkey Hanuman. 'If you help us get back into our palace and throw *our* wicked king out, then we will get all our brilliant monkeys and bears together to help you find your Sita.'

And that is what they did. Ram helped Sugreev become the new Monkey King and Sugreev in turn called all his generals and instructed them to look north, south, east and west for Sita. 'And return in exactly one month with your reports,' added Sugreev.

It fell to Hanuman to accompany the Bear General of the South. As he was leaving, Ram said to him, 'Hanuman, I have great faith in you. If you find my Sita, show her this ring. Then she will know you are my messenger. Tell her I love her and that I will come for her soon.' Ram took off his ring and handed it to Hanuman.

The Northern Battalion searched in the snows of the Himalaya mountains and in the deep crevices where mighty rivers begin. They could not find Sita and returned in a month.

The Eastern Battalion searched in thick bamboo forests and jungles filled with rhinoceroses. They did not find Sita and returned a month later.

The Western Battalion searched in rice fields and rocky coves. They did not find Sita and returned a month later.

The Southern Battalion searched through tall jackfruit trees and along meandering rivers that were lined with palms. They did not find Sita anywhere. Just as they were thinking of returning, they fell into a hole in a cave. Struggling out of it with great difficulty they found themselves on a beach.

A very discouraged Hanuman asked the Bear General, 'We have now reached the southern tip of this land. There is nothing ahead of us but the ocean. How many days has it been since we left our King?'

'It has been a month and a day,' replied the Bear General.

'A month and *a day*! This is a disgrace! We should have been back by now. We are a day late. And what is worse, we have no good news.'

'Well, I don't understand what all the fuss is about,' said the Bear General, 'I'm exhausted.' With that he lay down on the beach, and as if commanded, the rest of the army stretched out as well.

'How did all this mess get started anyway?' asked the Bear General.

Hanuman, who by this time, had rested his head on the bear's stomach started to tell him the story of Ram.

They were interrupted by the sudden arrival of an old vulture who could not fly too well. It landed on the sand with such a thud that it created a sandstorm and buried most of the animal soldiers up to their necks.

'My dinner is all laid out for me,' exclaimed the vulture, seeing all those delicious heads popping out of the sand.

Hanuman, who was still telling Ram's story, had just reached the part about the Vulture King.

'Why are you talking about my brother?' asked the vulture.

'Oh, so he was your brother, was he?' said Hanuman and began to tell his story all over again.

As he reached the end the vulture suddenly interrupted. 'Wait a minute! I have exquisite eyesight. And *I* am certain that I saw Ravan taking Sita over this ocean to his kingdom of Lanka.'

'You did!? Oh, this is sweet music to our ears. Now we can continue our search towards Lanka and find out where Sita is hidden.'

'But how will we cross the ocean?' asked the Bear General. 'The island is supposed to be a hundred leagues away.'

'Let us call all the apes, monkeys, chimpanzees and bears in our army and see who can leap the farthest,' suggested Hanuman.

'I can leap twenty five leagues,' said a small squirrel monkey.

'I can do thirty-five leagues,' said a black, furry bear.

'That's nothing. I can do a hundred leagues,' boasted Hanuman.

'Then why don't *you* go? That is the exact distance required,' said the Bear General.

'Did I er . . . actually say I could jump a hundred leagues?' asked Hanuman.

'Yes. Now I am ordering you to jump.'

Hanuman took one look at the blue ocean. It seemed as vast as the blue sky. He then closed his eyes, breathed deeply, crouched . . . and leapt into the air.

V The Siege of Lanka

HANUMAN LANDED RIGHT IN THE MIDDLE of Lanka. 'I am quite wonderful,' he said aloud. 'Not a monkey hair out of place. What a leap! What a leap!'

The high walls of Lanka city were surrounded by a deep moat that was filled with killer sharks. The brick-lined streets were graced on either side with tall mansions and stately trees. Everywhere there were demons—some green, some pink, some black and some quite transparent. Some were hideous and others were as beautiful as anything in heaven.

But where was Sita to be found?

Hanuman scampered quietly over a high fence and found himself in a large garden. Nearby he could hear some ugly demons talking to each other.

'We could gobble this Sita up in a minute if it were not for King Ravan's instructions,' said one female.

'You idiot, we are supposed to be guarding her, not eating her. Besides, Ravan wants to marry her,' said another.

'Why does he wait for her consent when he can take her by force?' said the first.

'Don't you know about the curse? If he takes any woman by force, he is cursed to die. That is why he must be patient. It can't be long now. She can't say "no" forever.'

Hanuman's hair stood on end. Poor, poor Sita, he thought. He must find her.

He followed the two demons to a tall, flowering tree. There, underneath it, sitting in a huddle, was the most beautiful human creature Hanuman had ever seen. He clambered up the tree and sat hidden in its branches until the demons were gone.

Then he dropped Ram's ring into Sita's lap.

Sita looked up, quite startled.

'Don't be discouraged, brave Sita,' Hanuman whispered. 'I am Ram's messenger. I will tell him where you are and he will rescue you.'

Sita gave Hanuman a pearl she always wore and said, 'Give this to Ram. Tell him I love him.'

But demons are very clever. They could smell an intruder in their city. They hunted Hanuman down and bound him up. Then they tied rags to his tail, dipped the rags in oil, and set them on fire.

'There, monkey,' they said, 'that will teach you to spy on our land!'

Hanuman flew around Lanka with his tail blazing. He touched one mansion with it and it caught on fire. He touched another, and another and another. Half of Lanka was ablaze before Hanuman dipped his tail into the ocean to cool it off. Then he stretched his muscles and snapped off all the ropes that bound him.

He took another giant leap over the ocean and was back home. He gave

Sita's pearl to Ram and told his story, adding, 'Let us prepare our armies for war. Sita is waiting for us.'

Hundreds and thousands of bears and monkeys collected their weapons and began the long march to the ocean.

When the waves touched their feet they stopped. How would an entire army cross the ocean?

Just then, the Ocean King rose up from the waters and said, 'There is amongst you a monkey who spends his idle hours skimming stones over the water. Let him step forward.'

A small, fat brown monkey took one step forward. 'Here, sir,' he said.

'You skim your stones over the water from here to Lanka and I will make sure that the stones keep floating. This way, you will have a bridge,' said the Ocean King.

The fat, brown monkey began skimming his stones. A bridge began to grow.

When the squirrels in the trees saw what was happening, they said, 'We will help too. We want to help the good Prince Ram.' They came out from bushes, out from treetrunks and out from the branches of shady trees. First they jumped into the water to wet their fur, then they rolled in the sand and then they ran up the stone bridge and shook off their sand. They did this again and again until the bridge to Lanka looked like a paved road.

King Ravan looked out of the top window in his palace and saw a bridge advancing towards Lanka.

'Fools,' he muttered, 'we'll kill them all as they land. I'll talk to my brothers.'

Ravan's First Brother said, 'Ram is a good man. Don't fight him. You cannot possibly win. Return his wife to him. That is all he asks for. Spare our nations unnecessary bloodshed.'

'You cowardly fool,' said Ravan, 'I'll keep Sita *and* defeat her puny husband. I don't need your help. Get out.'

So Ravan's First Brother left Lanka and joined Ram's forces.

Ravan's Second Brother, was a giant who slept for six months and then woke up for just a day. It was his day to rise and shine.

'Go light a fire under my Second Brother to hasten his waking up,' Ravan said. 'And have a meal ready. A hundred crisply roasted buffaloes, two hundred cartfuls of rice, and five hundred vats of the best wine. Hurry. Meanwhile, ask my generals to begin the attack.'

When Ravan reached his Second Brother, he found him barely up.

'I want you to prepare for war,' said Ravan.

'Whatever for?' the Second Brother yawned so hard that he sucked in all the birds that were flying around his palace. 'I've just woken up. I hate all these earthly problems. That is why I prefer to sleep.'

'Ram is here to get his wife back. You may have to fight him,' Ravan said.

'Wouldn't it be simpler if you just returned his wife?' asked his giant brother.

'I would rather die first,' said Ravan.

Just then Ravan's servants came to him to announce that his generals were

dead, slain by Ram's army.

'Oh well,' said Ravan's Second Brother. 'I suppose I'll have to fight now. I will willingly kill them and drink their blood. I must say, though, that stealing another man's wife is absolutely wrong.'

So the giant brother went out to fight. War drums and trumpets pierced the air as he moved on Ram's army of animals like a towering war machine, spitting arrows in all directions. The little monkeys and little bears were terrified and fled in all directions. The brave Hanuman leapt up and took a bite out of the giant brother's ear. It did not do much good. Finally, Ram aimed a careful arrow and shot off the giant's head. The arrow was so fierce that it carried the Second Brother's head over the city of Lanka, drenching it with blood.

Next, Ravan sent his son, Indrajit, to fight. Drums and trumpets sounded again. The son, using his father's chariot of the skies, circled Ram's army and let loose a storm of thunderbolts, spears and serpent darts.

By nightfall, every member of Ram's army lay wounded.

Indrajit reported to his father, 'They are all finished. My dearest father, from now on you will have no more worries.'

Meanwhile, on the battlefield, the Bear General was crying, 'Medicine, medicine, we need medicine. We must have medicine tonight.'

The Bear General saw that Hanuman had some strength left. 'Go,' he ordered, 'go to the Himalaya Mountains tonight. Bring back healing herbs from the Magic Mountain.'

Hanuman closed his eyes, bent his knees, took a deep, deep breath, and leapt. Before he knew it, he was in the Himalaya Mountains.

But it was pitch dark and he could not tell one herb from another.

'Bother!' he said. 'I'll just take the whole mountain.'

Holding the mountain aloft in one hand he leapt back to Lanka. As he hovered over the army, he shouted, 'Where shall I put this down? Hurry. Hurry. Make some space below. This thing is heavy, make room.'

'There is no room here for such a huge mountain,' said the Bear General. 'The aromas from the herbs have revived our army, so you can take the mountain back.'

Next day, Ravan heard sounds of rejoicing coming from the animal army. 'What on earth is going on?' he asked.

His spies climbed up on the walls of the city and did not like what they saw.

'The animal army has recovered and is besieging the city,' they reported to Ravan.

'How can that be?' said a bewildered Ravan, shaking all his ten heads. 'This is not possible.'

Then Ravan's son, Indrajit, spoke up. 'Do not worry, father, I am still here. I will take care of this.'

Indrajit tightened his belt and put on his gleaming silver armour. As he stepped outside the walls of his city, he called, 'Laxshman, you may have survived my last attack but this time I will finish you. I challenge you to a duel.'

'I accept the challenge,' Laxshman yelled back.

The two went at each other with every weapon they had. Indrajit threw a poisoned javelin at Laxshman, who cut it into small pieces with his arrow. Indrajit lifted his bow and shot off a thousand arrows. Laxshman stopped each arrow with one of his own. Indrajit lifted up his sword and came at Laxshman.

'Enough is enough,' said Laxshman. He took slow, careful aim with his bow and, using a single arrow, shot off Indrajit's head.

When Ravan heard of this, he let out a yell of pain. 'My son, my dear son, dead! It is unbearable. I am the most unfortunate man alive. My generals are dead, my dear Second Brother is gone, and now my son, my son, my dear, dear son.'

That night it was very quiet. The stars shone clearly and brightly in the sky.

All the next day Ravan and his demons prepared again for war — a war to the death.

Ravan put on his gold armour and all his ten gold helmets. In the dark of the night Ravan and his demons thundered across Lanka's drawbridge and advanced towards the army waiting below.

Ram said to his army of animals, 'All my friendly monkeys and bears, take cover and hide. This is my battle.' He turned to his brother Laxshman, and said, 'You go with them. This is a fight I must fight alone.'

His army fell back.

There was a glow in the sky. Ravan was approaching in his chariot. Ram climbed into a chariot of his own and rushed towards the oncoming enemy.

They fought with golden arrows and silver spears. If Ravan shot a million arrows at him, Ram countered with a million of his own. If Ravan's twenty arms aimed twenty spears at Ram, Ram sloughed them all off with his shield. Each man stood tall in his chariot. The clash of weapons resounded through earth and heaven. Ravan swung a mace round and round, letting it gather power and speed, and then he hurled it at Ram. Ram ducked to one side and let if fly past him. Then Ram aimed a single arrow at Ravan. It broke Ravan's shield and struck Ravan in the centre of his heart. Ravan was dead. All the demons fled in fear. The animals jumped up and down shouting 'Glory be to Ram. Glory be to Ram.'

It was daybreak. Hanuman went scampering off to Sita to give her the good news. 'I still have the jewels you threw down to earth when Ravan was carrying you away,' he said.

Sita put the jewels on and combed her hair. 'How is my husband?' she asked.

'Come with me and you will find out,' Hanuman said. 'Laxshman has built a small hut of leaves for you so that you may rest.'

Hanuman led Sita to her waiting husband.

'Oh my Sita, what you must have suffered,' said Ram embracing her.

He put his arm around her shoulders and led her to the hut.

Meanwhile, the animal army began preparations to return home.

And Laxshman prepared to return to Ayodhya, where his brother would be crowned king.

The fourteen years of exile were over.

THE DAY OF
THE WINTRY FULL MOON

Have you ever tried to thread a needle by moonlight? That is what my mother and grandmother made me do when I was little.

There was a good reason for it, so they said.

In the early evening of a special full moon night that fell in the clear, cool month of October, my mother would hitch up her sari and tuck its flowing end neatly into her waist. With beads of perspiration collecting on the tip of her short, button nose she would roast mounds of semolina in a big frying pan, shaking the large pan expertly until a nutty aroma filled the kitchen. To this semolina, she added sugar, nuts and clarified butter and then she spread the mixture in round trays to form a halva. All the children were pressed into service, carrying the trays up the steep stone steps to the roof.

As night fell, we waited on the roof with the trays. The night got colder and colder and the moon brighter and brighter. It was then that we, as instructed by the women below, took out our needles and began threading them, again and again, until we had done it one hundred and ten times.

Why?

Because this special full-moon night in October is a night of magic. It is the night when the moonbeams carry not just the most brilliant rays of light, but tiny droplets of Amrit, heavenly nectar that can make a person immortal.

If we were lucky, and the nectar hit our eyes as we caught the light to thread our needles, then our eyes would shine clearly and brightly for the rest of our lives. If we were luckier still, and the nectar went past our lips, then we would surely never die.

If the moonbeams missed our eyes and missed our lips, they are bound to glance off the trays of semolina halva and transfer to it all the goodness of the moon. Then we could eat the halva and gobble up the best of the moon.

There is a story about the Moon and the Heavenly Nectar.

The Moon
and the
Heavenly Nectar

WHEN THE WORLD WAS FORMED, the Creator of the Universe churned the mighty oceans to see what they might throw up.

The oceans then were filled with milk and popping out of them, like rocks from a volcano, came massive rubies, diamonds, emeralds and sapphires.

Out of the churning also came the Heavenly Nectar of Immortality and Poison.

When the Poison came out, it was accompanied by much fuming and hissing. The milky ocean immediately turned to salt water. The god Shiva, wanting to protect the world, took the Poison and put it in his throat, which is why his neck is always as blue as the wings of a shining butterfly.

Everyone wanted the Nectar of Immortality. At that time, there were no human beings, only gods and demons, who immediately began squabbling over it.

Vishnu, the Creator and Preserver, was watching all this from the heavens and decided it was time to step in. In his thunderous voice, he called out:

'All you gods and demons, tonight I will decide the question of immortality once and for all. Let us all meet at midnight.'

When they all met that night, Vishnu came disguised as a beautiful maiden and in his arms he carried the jug of nectar. He asked the gods and demons to sit in a row and when he passed a demon, he flirted with him and fluttered his eyelashes to distract him. When he passed a god, he quickly gave him a sip of nectar, for it was his intention that only the gods should become immortal.

However, he made one mistake.

As he passed Rahu, the evil star, he raised the jug of nectar to offer him a sip.

Fortunately the Moon was watching and he sent out a quick beam towards Vishnu with the message, 'Watch out for Rahu, the Demon.'

But it was too late. A single drop of nectar had already passed Rahu's lips. Vishnu, greatly upset at what he had done, drew his sword and cut off Rahu's head.

But Rahu had already swallowed a drop of nectar and he did not die.

He yelled furiously at the Moon, 'I saw you betraying me and I will have my revenge. You may shine brightly, just as you please, but once every year I will wipe that smile and that bright light off your face.'

And that is why, once a year, there is an eclipse of the Moon.

If you listen hard enough, that is the day you can hear Rahu laughing.

KARVACHAUTH– THE LITTLE CLAY POT

As a child I never stopped to question why it was that my mother fasted and prayed once a year for God to give long life to my father and why my father never did the same for her. If, at that age, I had asked my mother this question, I am sure her answer would have been, 'Because that is the way it *is*.'

In India, life is set up to follow certain pre-arranged patterns. No one knows exactly who decided on these patterns or when they were decided upon. But somewhere, sometime, it was decided that married Hindu women would set aside a day to pray for their husbands. The day, called Karvachauth, would be in the autumn, on the fourth day of the moon. So, ever since anybody can remember, married women have been following this pattern without questioning it. I know that in the case of my mother, she followed it partly because tradition demanded it, partly because she loved the fuss and details of religious ceremonies—but mainly because she adored my father and was not going to take any chances on his health and longevity!

At night we all slept in a row on a back verandah which faced the rose and jasmine garden. Even though we slept on beds next to each other, we were really quite isolated, as each bed was enshrouded by a large, white mosquito-net, held up by four bamboo poles. My father slept at one end, with my mother next to him, then my baby-sister, me and my two older sisters. I did have two older brothers as well, but at the age of seven, they were shady figures, who seemed always to be away at a distant school or on fishing trips.

Since married women were supposed to fast from sunrise, my mother would set the alarm for four o'clock in the morning. This would allow her to get a quick bite to eat before sunrise. She was perfectly willing to follow the required rules about fasting and praying on the day of Karvachauth itself—but no rule said that she couldn't spend the last minute of the previous day eating all she needed to sustain her! As the alarm went off, my father would stir and grumble. He would then pull the quilt over his head and go back to sleep. My mother would emerge from her mosquito-net, awaken any of her daughters who had so requested, and begin to brush her teeth vigorously with a twig from a neem tree which she always kept at a nearby table. My sisters and I were awakened because we insisted upon it. We wanted to watch every bit of the ritual connected with this special day. My mother, with her daughters following behind her like ducklings, would go to the pantry where food had been left warming for her from the previous night. As my mother ate some sauced potatoes and deep-fried breads we would sit around and watch her. Every now and then she would pop a bit of food from her plate into our mouths. This made us feel as if we were really participating. Perhaps at this strange hour between night and day my mother was quietly passing on a 'pattern' or a tradition from her generation to ours.

We were sent off to bed again and awakened just in time for school. My mother would braid our well-oiled hair and secure them with freshly ironed ribbons. Once we had breakfasted, we were packed off to school with khaki sun-hats on our heads and leather school-bags in our hands. The school-day would actually be quite normal but it *felt* special. I would run around whispering to the whole class, 'My mother is fasting today, you know. It's Karvachauth. It's very important that she fasts from sunrise until the first appearance of the moon. Otherwise my father will DIE.' Since most of the class was Christian, this bit of information would both alarm and impress them. The whole idea was to get even with my class-mates for the large Easter eggs they brought in annually, as well as for the pretty pastel holy pictures which they traded, bought and sold during every break between classes.

The rest of the school-day was spent day-dreaming—imagining my mother's activities . . . now, with her sari tucked between her legs, she must be standing in the kitchen frying those sweet, whole-wheat fritters! Since my sisters found them too doughy and sticky, I could look forward to eating their share as well! Bell after bell would ring at school, arithmetic books were exchanged for geography books, but my mind was at home.

By the time we got home from school and changed from our sweaty navy-blue tunics, white socks and tightly laced black shoes into loose Indian dresses and open sandals, my mother would be putting the finishing touches to the prayer-room—fresh flowers in the brass vases, straw mats on the floor and special little 'Karva' clay pots with lids and spouts filled with water, with the fresh fritters sitting on their lids.

While we waited for the moon to appear, my father would retire to the living-room, turn on the radio and listen to news of the Second World War over the BBC World Service. His wife and daughters would go into the prayer-room and begin praying for his health and long life.

We would all sit cross-legged on the mats, the candles and oil-lamps would be lit and the prayers would begin. The first and best part was The Story.

The Girl
Who Had
Seven Brothers

LONG, LONG AGO there was a large house in which lived seven brothers and their seven wives. The brothers had a young sister who shared their lodging and upon whom they doted. She was fifteen, and had long, black, wavy hair, soft doe-like eyes, a small rose-bud mouth and an infectious, lilting laugh. The brothers knew that it was time they arranged a marriage for their sister as she was now of age, but they hated the thought of parting with her, so whenever their wives began a discussion about her age and marital prospects, they successfully changed the subject.

When she was sixteen, the brothers, pushed and nagged by their wives, reluctantly agreed to arrange the marriage of their sister. They knew of a rich land-owner who lived two hundred miles to the East and who was reputed to be young and handsome. So they sent their sister's horoscope to him, set a match, and one brisk winter day, married their sister to this handsome youth.

As the days went by, the brothers began to miss their sister very much. Whenever they got too depressed, they would console themselves by telling each other that she was, after all, very much in love with her husband and that the match had worked out better than their own marriages and that her happiness was all that should matter.

Ten months passed without the brothers seeing their sister. Even though she wrote to them regularly, they missed her laughter and her gaiety. So they sent her an invitation to come with her husband and celebrate Karvachauth with them.

The big house was cleaned and decorated for the festival. The ladies started their fast and cooked the fritters, and the brothers stood near the front door waiting for their sister to arrive.

Their sister and her husband arrived around noon, on the day of Karvachauth. Although she still laughed and joked as she used to, the brothers were quick to notice that her face had an unusual pallor and that there were dark circles under her eyes. When they asked her about this she answered, 'Oh, it was such a long journey. We had intended to spend the night in a village along the way, but were so afraid of not being here in time, that we kept riding through the night. We have not slept, that's all. Besides, I'm fasting, as you know.' It was the truth but the over-anxious brothers kept worrying. 'Perhaps you should eat,' they said, 'You really look ill.' 'Don't be silly,' she answered, 'this is my first Karvachauth and I intend to keep the fast.' She looked so lovingly at her husband as she said this, that the brothers were forced to be quiet.

As the day wore on, the sister grew weaker. The brothers again suggested that she should eat and again she smiled and tossed her head saying, 'Certainly not.'

Night fell. The brothers scanned the skies for the moon but it was nowhere in sight. They went to their sister and said, 'The moon is out but there is a dark covering of clouds over it, so it cannot be seen. It is perfectly all right to eat now.' The sister looked out of the window and seeing no moon, said, 'I will eat only when I *see* the moon.'

Time passed and the sister lay weakly on a cot. The brothers could stand it no longer, so they devised a plan. One of them climbed a tall tree with an oil lamp in his hand. The others went into the kitchen and got a sieve, then they called their sister outdoors, crying, 'The moon is out, the moon is out.' They asked their sister to look through the sieve at the oil lamp on the tree-top. The poor girl, in her weakened condition, looked up at the tree and did indeed think she was seeing the moon. The brothers brought her some milk and some fritters which she ate thankfully. She then went indoors and told her sisters-in-law to eat as the moon was out. But they all looked at her coldly and said, 'Your moon may be out but ours is not.' At this, the girl became suspicious. She ran, stumbling, to the room where her husband was, only to find him lying dead on the floor. She screamed and wept and pleaded with the nine Earth Mothers, the goddesses of Karvachauth, to return her husband's life, but it was of no avail. The brothers, stricken with guilt, tried to console her but she pushed them away crying, 'I will carry my husband into the forest. There I will sit with his body for twelve full months. Next year, when the nine goddesses of Karvachauth pass through again, I will beg them to give life back to my husband.' So saying, she summoned all her energy and carried her husband's body deep into the forest. There, she sat with it in her lap for exactly one year.

The following year, on the day of Karvachauth, the first of the Earth Mothers appeared before the sister, dressed in pink and silver and wearing a big pearl nose-ring. Her face gleamed with beauty like the moon. As she approached the weeping girl, she said,

> 'Oh sister of seven brothers,
> You couldn't stay hungry
> And you couldn't stay thirsty.
> Come give me your Karva pot.'

The weeping girl looked up at this radiant apparition and cried, 'Please don't say that. Instead, give life to my husband and say what you are supposed to say, which is—O happily married woman, take my Karva pot and give me

76

yours.' But the first goddess only shook her head, saying, 'I cannot do as you ask. But my sister will be passing through soon. Speak to her.'

The girl waited and soon the second goddess came. She was dressed in green and gold and wore an emerald nose-ring. She was not as beautiful as the first goddess, as her eyes looked liked those of a fox. She said,

'O sister of seven brothers,
You couldn't stay hungry
And you couldn't stay thirsty.
Come give me your Karva pot.'

The girl wailed, 'Please don't say that. Instead, say what you are supposed to say, which is—O happily married woman, take my Karva pot and give me yours.' The second goddess shook her head, saying, 'I cannot do as you ask. But my sister will be passing through soon. Speak to her.'

Soon, the third goddess came. She wore yellow and had the face of a rat. Her words were the same as her sisters'. The fourth goddess wore purple and had the face of a toad; the fifth goddess wore red and had the face of a bat; the sixth goddess wore blue and had the face of a lizard; the seventh goddess wore grey and had the face of a scorpion; the eighth goddess wore black and had the face of a snake. Each goddess refused to help the poor girl and referred her to her next sister.

The girl was moaning desperately now. She heard a jingling of bells in the forest and was sure the last Earth Mother was at hand. Suddenly, from behind her, a most hideous apparition leaped out. It looked like nothing she had seen even in her worst nightmares. The creature had one eye placed haphazardly on a triangular face. The rest of the face consisted of puffy green cheeks and nine sharp, curved fangs. The body, looking more like a misshapen lump, was balanced on two webbed feet which were engaged in some gruesome dance round and round the poor girl who still sat with her husband's body in her lap. This horrible creature laughed and screeched and began the familiar chant,

'Oh sister of seven brothers,
You couldn't stay hungry
And you couldn't . . .'

But the girl did not let her finish. She clung to those ugly feet, wailing, 'I won't let you go until you give life to my husband and say what you are supposed to say, which is—O happily married woman, take my Karva pot and give me yours.'

The ninth goddess tried to pull her feet away, but the girl held on, sobbing and beating her head against the ground. Finally, the goddess, touched by the girl's determination, relented, and said, 'Let it be as you ask.'

There was a flash of lightning. The ugly creature had vanished and in its place stood the dazzling first goddess in pink and silver. She restored the girl's husband back to life, saying, 'Come exchange Karva pots with me.'

The two women sat opposite each other and as one said, 'O happily married woman, take my Karva pot,' the other answered with, 'O happily married woman, give me your Karva pot.' They said this again and again, nine times over.

Then the goddess got up to leave. As she left, she warned, 'If you want your husband to stay alive, then every year, on the day of Karvachauth, you must fast from sunrise until the moon appears—and remember to pray to the nine Earth Mothers.' So saying, she disappeared into the darkness of the forest. . . .

DIVALI—FESTIVAL OF LIGHTS

Lakshmi, the goddess of wealth and good fortune, lives with the stars in the sky but she loves to look down and see lights twinkling on earth as well. So, to please her, once a year on Divali day—which fell on a dark moonless day in November, we were in the habit of decorating the outside of our home with tiny oil lamps.

It was not just the outside that we decorated. Lakshmi demanded that the entire house sparkle with cleanliness and beauty. This kind of demand suited my father just perfectly. He enjoyed everything to do with improving the house. He used the time just before Divali not only to get the house painted but to add a room here, a courtyard there, and a verandah somewhere else. Divali, which came in late autumn, was, of course, the best time to do this. The monsoons were over and a brisk, sunny winter was about to begin.

Scores of workmen would descend upon the house and begin to scrape doors, window frames and walls. Meanwhile, we would all pore over shade charts, picking out different colours for different rooms. I remember one year, when I was about five, we picked the newest shade on the shade chart, mauve, for the children's study, with mouldings to be painted in gold.

I had never heard of the colour mauve before. I went around saying, 'mauve, mauve,' to the parrots that flew over our garden and to my friends who raced tricycles with me. The word was so new and exciting. When the study was finished, we were sure it would win Lakshmi's approval.

Divali day was a holiday for the whole country. While I tied a fresh ribbon in my hair, thousands of tiny oil lamps were lined along the parapet of our roof and on every window sill, doorway and ledge. Nothing was lit until after evening prayers—and after my mother had told us the Divali story. By this time it would be quite dark. We would run outside and begin lighting the lamps, one by one.

Soon the whole house would be glittering, as would our neighbour's house and the house next to that. The whole country was probably glittering, just like our neighbourhood. Then it was time for the fireworks. My father would aim a fiery rocket towards the sky. I would take a long sparkler, stand in the middle of the lawn and then turn round and round and round until I seemed encircled by my very own glow.

Lakshmi
and the Clever
Washerwoman

ONCE UPON A TIME, a king and queen lived in a beautiful palace. The Queen was rather spoiled and vain. Every Divali, she would ask her husband for the most expensive presents. Each year, the King gave her whatever she asked for, however difficult it was for him to get it.

One particular year, the Queen had asked for a seven-string necklace of large pearls.

The King sent a thousand divers to the far corners of the earth searching for those pearls. Just before Divali, the divers returned. They had, at great peril to their own lives, found just the right oysters and, from them, pulled out only those rare pearls that were large and perfect.

The grateful King thanked the divers profusely and gave them large sums of money for their labours. He sent the pearls to the royal jeweller to be strung and on Divali morning he was able to present his wife with the gift she desired.

The Queen was jubilant. She put on the necklace and immediately ran to the mirror to admire herself. She turned her head this way and that, convinced that she was, indeed, the most beautiful creature in the whole world.

It was the Queen's custom to go to the river every morning to bathe, accompanied by a bevy of handmaidens. On this particular morning when she got to the river bank, she undressed and, just as she was poised to dive into the water, she remembered that she was still wearing her seven-string necklace of pearls.

So she stopped and took it off, laying it on top of her clothes. 'Watch my necklace,' she called, as she dived off a rock.

The handmaidens watched the necklace carefully, but something happened which even they were unprepared for. A crow flew down from a nearby tree, picked up the necklace and flew away with it. The handmaidens screamed and shouted but it was no use. The crow had flown out of their sight.

When the Queen found out what had happened she cried with frustration and anger. She went back to the palace and, still sobbing, told the King of her misadventure. The King tried to console her, saying that he would get her a prettier necklace but the Queen pouted and said that she would not be happy until her seven-string necklace was found.

So the King summoned his drummers and heralds. He ordered them to go

to every town and village in the kingdom, telling the people that a reward would be offered to anyone who found the Queen's necklace.

Meanwhile, the crow had flown from the manicured palace grounds to one of the lowliest slum areas. Here he dropped the necklace on the doorstep of a poor washerwoman's hut.

The washerwoman did not live alone. She shared the hut with her constant companion, an old, toothless crone, called Poverty. The two were not particularly fond of each other but they had been together ever since the washerwoman could remember and had become quite used to each other's ways.

As it happened, the two occupants of the hut were away when the crow flew by. The washerwoman was collecting dirty laundry and Poverty, as usual, was accompanying her. On their way home, they passed the village market where they stopped to hear the King's drummers and the proclamation about the Queen's necklace. Poverty began to cackle, 'Oh the ways of royalty! What will they lose next? Why do they bother us common people with their antics!'

But the washerwoman was thinking other thoughts. She had never owned any jewellery and wondered how she would look in a seven-string necklace.

When they got home and the washerwoman put her bundles down, the first thing she noticed was the pearl necklace lying on her doorstep. She picked it up and was about to put it on when a thought occurred to her. 'I have an errand to run,' she told Poverty, 'I will be back in a minute.' So saying, she rushed off with the necklace and headed straight for the King's palace.

The guards tried to stop her but when she told them what she was carrying, they escorted her directly to the King.

The King was very happy to get his wife's necklace back. He praised the washerwoman for her honesty and then, picking up a large purse containing the reward money, he said, 'Here, take this for your pains. It should keep you well fed and well clothed for the rest of your days.'

To his surprise, the King found himself being refused. The washerwoman seemed to have something else in mind. She said, 'I am a poor, humble washer-woman, Your Majesty. I do not want the money which you are so kindly offer-ing me. There is one favour, however, that I hope you will grant me. Today is Divali. I want you to decree that no one, not even you, will light any oil lamps in his home. Today I want all houses to be dark. All except mine. I want mine to be the only lighted house in the entire kingdom.'

The King, grateful that he had got off so lightly, agreed. He sent out his drummers and heralds with the decree as he had promised. He ordered his palace servants to take down all the oil lamps and to put them into storage for the following year.

The washerwoman rushed home, buying as many oil lamps along the way as she could afford. She arranged these carefully outside her hut and waited.

Night fell. The washerwoman lit all her lamps and looked around. The rest of the kingdom to the north, south, east and west, lay in total darkness.

Lakshmi had, of course, left the heavens and was ready to perform her yearly duty of going from house to house, blessing with prosperity all those that were well lit. This year, something was wrong. There were no lights to be seen anywhere. Poor Lakshmi stumbled along in the darkness, from one house to another, but nowhere could she see the slightest trace of a welcoming glimmer.

Suddenly she spotted a glow of bright lights far away in the distance. She began running towards it.

It was the middle of the night when a very exhausted Lakshmi got to the washerwoman's hut. She began pounding on the door, crying, 'Let me in, let me in!'

This was the moment that the washerwoman had been waiting for. She called out to Lakshmi, saying, 'I will let you in only on the condition that you stay with me for seven generations.' Just then, the washerwoman looked behind her and saw Poverty trying to creep out through the back door. She rushed to the door and locked it. Poverty began to shout, 'Let me out, let me out!' You know there isn't room in this hut for both Lakshmi and me.'

So the washerwoman said, 'All right, I will let you go but only on the condition that you do not return for seven generations.' Poverty said, 'Yes, yes, I will do as you ask. Just let me out of this place. I cannot stand the sight of Lakshmi.' At that the washerwoman opened the back door and Poverty rushed out.

Then she hurried to the front door where Lakshmi was pounding desperately and crying, 'Let me in, let me in.'

'Only on the condition that you stay with me for seven generations,' the washerwoman repeated.

'Yes, yes,' said Lakshmi, 'I will do anything you ask, only let me in.'

And so the poor washerwoman let Lakshmi into her home and it was blessed with wealth and prosperity for seven generations.

HOLI—FESTIVAL OF SPRING

Holi is the Indian Spring Festival, a time when winter crops, such as wheat and mustard seeds, are harvested.

I cannot tell you how much I looked forward to this festival. In fact, I longed for it a good three hundred and sixty-four days of the year.

The reason was that our whole family did *such* unusual things to celebrate Holi.

First of all, on the day of the full moon around late February or early March, we built a huge bonfire. This was called 'burning Holi', because on this day, ages ago, a wicked princess, Holika, was consumed by flames that she had intended for her innocent nephew Prahlad.

Frankly, I cared less for Holika, who was burnt in ancient history, than I did for the stuff we actually threw into our own bonfire. We threw whole sheafs of green wheat, whole bundles of green chickpeas, still on their stalks, pinecones filled with strategically hidden pinenuts, and then watched them as their skins got charred.

Only the outside skins were allowed to burn. That was the trick. Each one of us then used a stick to pull out whatever we wanted to eat. My favourite was the chickpeas—tiny chickpeas still in their green skins. Of course, the skins would turn brownish-black but the peas themselves would be deliciously roasted. Everything would be hot—we would almost burn our fingers trying to peel the chickpeas and remove the shells from the pinenuts. Their taste would have to last us for the rest of the year as we licked our lips and remembered. By the end of it all, our faces were black and our clothes and hands were sooty, but no one seemed to mind, not even our parents.

The funny thing about Holi was that we could 'burn' it one night and 'play' it the next morning. While the 'burning' had to do, naturally, with fire, the 'playing' had to do with water and colours.

It was said that Lord Krishna, the blue god, played Holi with the milkmaids, so who were we to do any less?

As the Spring Festival approached, an army of us young cousins would, in great secrecy and in competing groups, begin its preparation of colours.

At Holi, all Indians, of all ages, have the license to rub or throw colours—waterbased, oil-based or in powder form—on the victims of their choice. No one is considered worthy of exemption, dignified grandmothers included.

Holi is a leveller, and there was no one we wanted to level more than those against whom we held grudges. A special ugly colour was prepared for them.

First, we would go to the garage and call on one of the chauffeurs.

'Masoom Ali? Masoom Ali?' we would call.

Masoom Ali would poke his head out from the pit under the gleaming Ford. 'I am busy. Why are you children always disturbing me? Always coming here to eat my head. Barrister Sa'ab, your grandfather, wants the car at noon and I still have much work to do.'

'Just give us some of the dirtiest grease from under the car.'

'So, Holi is upon us again? Why don't you children use the normal red, green and yellow colours?'

'If you give us the grease, we won't spray you with the awful magenta paint we have prepared in the garden watertank. It is a fast colour, too.'

'Threatening an old man, are you! All right, all right. Just don't eat my head.'

The grease would be combined with mud, slime and permanent purple dye. The concoction would be reserved for the lowliest enemies. Elderly relatives got a sampling of the more dignified, store-bought powders, yellow, red and green. For our best friends, we prepared a golden paint, carefully mixing real gilt and oil in a small jar. This expensive colour, would, as I grew older, be saved only for those members of the opposite sex on whom I had the severest crushes—transforming them, with one swift application, into golden gods.

The Wicked King
and his
Good Son

HIRANYA KASHYAP thought very highly of himself. He was good looking, rich—and he was the King. What more could anyone want? One day, a wise Sage, who could see into the past and the future, came to him and said, 'Your majesty, according to what I see in the stars, you cannot be killed by man, beast or weapons, during the day or during the night, on earth or in water, inside a house or, indeed, outside it.'

That, as far as King Hiranya Kashyap was concerned, made him immortal. If he was arrogant before, he now became unbearable and was very cruel to those subjects who did not flatter him endlessly. If he said, 'This bread is stale,' all his palace cooks would have to agree and throw it out, even if they had just cooked it. If he said, 'The River Ganges flows up from the sea to the Himalaya Mountains,' all the courtiers would have to nod their heads in agreement even though they knew that the Ganges began as a series of cool, icy trickles from the cracks of the world's highest mountains and then flowed, slowly and gracefully, down to the sea.

The sad fact of the matter was that Hiranya Kashyap thought he was God. Not only did he make his subjects kneel and pray to him but he bullied and tortured those who did not.

He had a sister called Holika who had been told by the same wise Sage that she could never be burnt by fire. Hiranya Kashyap and Holika became so vain that they behaved as if they were owners of the entire universe.

Then, one day, all this changed.

Hiranya Kashyap's wife gave birth to a baby boy whom they named Prahlad.

Hiranya Kashyap found no need, or time, to rejoice.

When the courtiers came to him and said, 'Congratulations, your majesty, on the birth of your heir,' he only snarled, saying, 'Bah, what do I need an heir for? I shall live forever. I am God. Heirs mean nothing to me.'

One day, when Prahlad was four, he was playing outside the potter's kiln and saw the potter praying.

'What are you doing?' he asked.

'I am praying to God to save my kittens,' she replied. 'They have got locked up in the kiln by accident.'

'You should pray to my father,' said Prahlad.

'Your father cannot save my kittens from that awful fire inside,' she said, 'only God can.'

'My father will punish you if you use God's name,' Prahlad advised her.

'I'll have to take my chances,' the potter replied.

'Your God can do nothing to help,' Prahlad said.

'Oh yes he can,' the potter answered.

'Then I'll wait here and see,' the young boy said. Prahlad waited. When it was time to open the kiln, he heard, 'Meaow, meaow.' It was the kittens. They were safe!

A year later, when Prahlad was five and was playing in the garden, his father chanced to pass that way. The King paused long enough to ask his son, 'Who is the greatest being in the whole Universe?' He expected the same answer he got from all his flatterers.

'God,' said the child.

The King was taken aback for a second. Then he smirked, 'See, see,' he boasted to his courtiers, 'even this small child recognizes that I am God.'

'No,' said the child, 'you are not God. You are the King and that is all you will ever be.'

Hiranya Kashyap's face turned purple with rage. 'Take this child,' he ordered, 'and hurl him from the highest cliff in the kingdom.'

The courtiers were very fond of the gentle child but were terrified of his father. So they scooped little Prahlad up and carried him to the highest mountain in the Himalayas. There, they stood on a peak that touched the sky and dropped the boy.

Prahlad fell . . . fell . . . fell. But to his surprise—and to that of the courtiers looking down from above—he landed in the midst of the warmest, sweetest softness that could be imagined. God had been watching from his heavenly window and had decided to catch the child in his lap.

When Hiranya Kashyap found out what had happened, he turned black with anger. He had the boy brought to the court and thrown at his feet.

'You were very lucky to be saved,' he raged.

'It was God who saved me,' Prahlad replied.

'As I was saying,' the King continued angrily, 'you were lucky to land in such a soft patch. The courtiers who threw you down there will have their heads chopped off and then I'm going to have a roaring fire made and have you burnt in it. Let us see what your God can do for you then!'

The King commanded that a huge bonfire be made the following day. Logs were collected and piled into a massive pyre. Then the pyre was lit.

Hiranya Kashyap called his sister, Holika, and said, 'If we just toss this child into the fire, he will squirm and run out. Since you have been granted the boon of never being burnt by fire, why don't you take Prahlad in your arms, walk into the flames and sit down. Hold the child tightly. When he is quite dead, you can walk out.'

Holika took Prahlad in her arms and walked into the middle of the fire.

There, she put him in her lap and sat down.

The flames were leaping hundreds of feet into the sky. Hiranya Kashyap was quite pleased with himself. He was finally getting rid of this troublesome child.

The flames were very hot and made the King perspire. At first he contented himself with moving back a few yards. Then, when the heat and smoke became quite overwhelming, he said to his courtiers, 'I'm going into my cool palace. Let me know when all this is over.'

A strange thing happened amidst the flames. Holika had a change of heart. She looked up towards heaven and prayed, 'God, please do not save me from the fire. I am ready to meet my Maker. But please save this innocent life. I give my boon to this young boy. Let him live.'

The fire burnt for several hours. The King had just sat down to enjoy his dinner when one of his courtiers came running in.

'Your majesty,' he said, bowing, 'your majesty.'

'Yes, yes, what is it. You know I do not like being disturbed at dinner time.'

'The fire has burned itself out.'

'And?' prompted the King.

'Holika has perished in the flames.'

'What!' cried the King, 'And the child?'

'Your majesty . . . Well, your majesty . . .'

'Well, what? Answer quickly or I'll have your tongue pulled out.'

'Prahlad is still alive.'

Hiranya Kashyap kicked his food away and stood on his feet, puffed up with fury like a balloon.

'Bring that brat to me. I'll kill him myself.'

The courtiers dragged in little Prahlad and threw him in front of his father.

'So,' said the father, 'you managed to escape a second time.'

'I did not escape,' said Prahlad, 'God saved me.'

'God, God,' cried the King, 'I'm sick of your God. Where is he anyway?'

'He is everywhere—in fire, water—even in that pillar.'

'Oh, he is in that pillar, is he?' the King yelled. 'Well, I am going to tie you up to that same pillar and kill you. Let's see if your God will come out to save you.'

Prahlad was tied up to the pillar and Hiranya Kashyap raised his sword to finish him off. Just then, there was a loud thunderclap and the pillar broke in two.

Out of the pillar came God.

He had assumed a strange shape.

The upper part of the body was that of a lion, the lower that of a man.

So he was neither man nor beast.

He lifted the King and carried him to the threshold of the palace and then placed him in his lap.

So the King was neither in a house nor outside it.

Then he killed Hiranya Kashyap with one swipe of his long lion's claws.
So no weapon was used.
The time of the day was dusk.
So it was neither morning nor night.
Pink and grey clouds puffed along in the sky. Hiranya Kashyap was finally dead, despite all his arrogant predictions.

The courtiers cried, 'Long live the King' as they placed the young Prahlad on his father's throne, happy in the knowledge that they were now going to be ruled with justice.

A DAY FOR BROTHERS

Some time around March, when the moon is in the second day of its waning cycle, all sisters in India pray that no harm comes to their brothers. If one lives in a large family as I did, one prays for one's male cousins as well. I rather enjoyed all this. I liked my brothers and cousins, all of whom happened to be older than I was. I had much to learn from them—fishing, for example.

Until I was four, I was only allowed to watch the boys collect and prepare their fishing gear. It all seemed an exotic male ritual of which I could never be a part. I could stand under the tamarind tree and watch a cousin dig for earthworms. I was not allowed to dig myself. I could watch lead weights being attached to fishing lines to make them sink and four-inch pieces of cane attached to them to make them float. I longed to join in this male world and ended up pushing hard for an invitation.

One year in March, when the icy winds had stopped swooping down on Delhi from the distant Himalaya mountains and when all the woollen clothes had been cleaned, folded and tucked into mothballed trunks, I approached a group of male cousins as they were preparing for their first fishing trip of the year. Their ages ranged from six to eleven. I was five.

'May I come with you this time, please?'

'No.'

'Why?'

'Because you're a girl.'

'But I can do everything you can.'

'No you can't. Why did you scream so much yesterday when we were digging up earthworms?'

'Because you cut an earthworm in half with your spade . . . and both halves were wriggling.'

'These things happen. None of the boys screamed.'

'I'll get used to it. Please let me come fishing with you.'

They relented eventually. My eldest cousin actually made me a small rod out of the cut-up bamboo. To this he attached a line made out of twine and a hook made out of a bent pin. I thought it best to put on a pair of shorts.

The Yamuna River was behind our house and it took us but five minutes to get to it. Once there, the boys spread themselves out on the rocks, threaded earthworms onto their hooks, and threw in their lines.

'Go on, go on, don't just sit there stupidly,' said my youngest cousin. 'Put your earthworm on and fish.'

How could I tell him that I was terrified of earthworms? I had never even touched one. I closed my eyes and put my fingers into the tin of worms. I could feel a wet, slimy tangled mass of creatures in there. I pulled one out. It felt quite awful. With my teeth clamped tightly so they would not open to let out the screech that was inside me, I began threading the creature onto the hook. First, the head, then bit by bit, the body. All was going well until I noticed some muddy stuff oozing out of the back of the worm. My teeth unclenched. I must have screeched for five whole minutes.

My eldest cousin put his arm around me and calmed me down. 'Never mind, never mind,' he said. 'I'll thread the worm for you. It takes a little while to get used to it. You will be just fine on the next fishing trip. Now do you want to hold my rod for a while?'

Some cousins and brothers can be so very nice. That is why I did not mind praying for them on the Day for Brothers. Here are two of the stories we were told that day.

The
Mango
Tree

IN A SMALL TOWN, there was a small house in which lived a young man, his wife, and the young man's sister. This small house had a small garden at the back in which grew a small mango tree. One day the young man's wife came to him and said, 'Look here, I'm fed up with our situation. Your sister . . .'

'Have you come here to complain about my sister again?'

'What can I do? I know it's quite useless . . . My complaints fall on deaf ears, anyway . . . I'm just . . . so angry with your sister. I get up early in the morning, draw water from the well, light the fire in the kitchen, cook breakfast, wash and scrub pots. . .'

'Don't go on,' said the brother. 'I've heard it all before.'

'And what does your lazy sister do all day? Nothing . . . nothing . . . she lolls about in the garden, watering her mango tree, talking to it, clearing away dead leaves, and feeding it manure and mulch. . .'

'That isn't all she does. She comes in and talks to me. Just an hour ago, she was playing chess with me.'

'Just because she adores you, doesn't mean you should ignore her faults. You must tell her to leave that . . . silly mango tree alone, and come and help me with the housework. I really think we should marry her off. That might teach her to be a bit more responsible.'

Since the sister was of marriageable age, the brother could not really object. He knew though, that he would miss her very, very much.

A marriage was arranged. When all the ceremonies were over, and the sister was about to leave with her groom to lead a new life in a new town, she turned to her sister-in-law and said, 'Dearest sister-in-law, I'm going to miss my mango tree so much. Would you please do me a great favour and look after it for me? Please water it well and clear the weeds that grow in its shadow.'

'Oh, well, yes, yes,' answered the sister-in-law.

Once the sister had left, the sister-in-law turned to her husband and yelled, 'Did you hear that? Did you *hear* that? Did you hear your selfish sister? She didn't say that she was going to miss you. She didn't say that she was going to miss me. She *did* say that she was going to miss her mango tree!' She decided then that she was going to ignore the mango tree. The mango tree irritated her just as much as her husband's sister had. Now she could be rid of both.

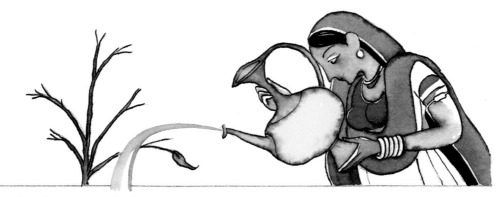

As the days passed, the unwatered, uncared for mango tree started drying up and its leaves began to fall.

At the same time, the brother, who had been a strong, robust and healthy young man, began to lose his appetite and get thinner and weaker.

One day, a letter arrived. It was from the sister and said, 'Dearest brother and sister-in-law. I hope all is well and that my tree is green and that my brother is in good health.'

The remaining leaves of the mango tree were quite yellow by this time, but the sister-in-law wrote back, 'Dearest sister. Your tree is fine, but your brother has not been feeling so good.'

Soon another letter arrived from the sister. 'Are you sure my tree is green? And how is my brother?'

The mango tree only had one brown leaf left on it now, and the brother was so sick that the doctors had said that he could not live. So the sister-in-law wrote back, 'Your tree is fine, but the doctors have given up all hopes for your brother.'

When the sister received this letter, she raced back to her small hometown and went straight into the small garden to water her small tree. As she watered it, cleared the weeds around it, and mulched it, it began slowly to turn green.

The brother too, began to recover.

As more leaves returned to the tree, the brother's cheeks got pinker and his eyes became brighter. Within a month, the tree was healthy and strong.

And so was the brother.

It was only then that the sister turned to her sister-in-law and said, 'Now do you understand? It was not the tree that I loved, but my brother. It was not the tree whose welfare I was concerned with, but my brother's. The tree and my brother share a common soul. It was my duty to look after them both.'

The
Faithful
Sister

HERE ONCE WAS A FAMILY with a single child—a shy girl who had to learn out of necessity to spend most of her time playing by herself. How she longed for a baby brother to play with.

But it was not to be until she was fifteen years old, when her mother gave birth to a boy and at the same time announced to her daughter that it was high time she was married. While the marriage was being arranged and prepared for, the girl spent most of her time with the new baby.

She would rock his cradle, kiss him and whisper, 'Oh, you dearest, sweetest brother, I love you so very much.'

Unfortunately, she was with her brother for only a year. Then she was married off to a man who lived quite far away.

The brother grew up knowing that he *had* a sister, but not knowing his sister at all.

The sister gradually had her own family but never stopped missing her dearest, sweetest brother.

When the brother was about to get married, he announced to his parents, 'I want to make sure that my sister attends my wedding. I will go to her home and invite her in person.'

When the brother arrived at his sister's house he knocked at her door.

He knocked and knocked and got no answer.

You see, it was the second day of the waning moon in March and the sister was praying for her brother. During these prayers, she was not supposed to talk.

So she could not come to the door.

The brother knocked and knocked and was just about to turn back when the sister appeared.

'Oh, dearest, sweetest brother,' she cried in joy, 'I am so very happy to see you. I couldn't answer the door earlier as I was praying for you. Please do come inside.'

'I cannot stay for long,' said the brother, 'I am soon to be married and came only to invite you. Why don't you return with me?'

'Oh my dearest, sweetest brother, of course I shall come to your wedding, but I will not leave for a few days. Stay for a while and eat and rest. I will cook you rice puddings and breads and sweets and also some extra food for you to take on your journey back home.'

The sister made all kinds of sweets, round ones and square ones and diamond shaped ones and squiggly ones for her brother to eat on his return trip. She tied them in a green cloth bundle and gave them to him.

After the brother had left, one of her children came to her and said, 'Mother, may I have some sweets?' She picked up a round sweet that she had not packed and broke it in two. She threw half of it to her dog—who promptly gobbled it up—and was just about to pop the other half into the mouth of her youngest child when the dog rolled over and died.

She quickly examined all the pots, pans and grinding stones in her kitchen and discovered to her horror that a poisonous snake had got into the bag of grain and that she had accidentally ground it when she was preparing her sweets.

She began to cry, 'Oh my dearest, sweetest brother. What have I done? What have I done? If you eat the sweets I gave you, you will die like my dog.'

She then rushed out of the house. Anyone she met on the road she would ask, 'Have you seen a traveller pass this way carrying a green bundle?' Every time she was told, 'Oh yes, such a traveller did pass this way. Just keep going and you'll reach him.'

So she went on running for hours and hours.

At last, she passed a blacksmith.

'Have you seen a traveller pass this way carrying a green bundle?' she asked.

'Oh yes,' said the blacksmith, 'such a traveller is sleeping under the mango tree further up the road.'

She found her brother and, hoping that he had not eaten the sweets, began shaking him. 'Wake up. Wake up. Don't die.'

The brother eventually sat up, 'What on earth are you saying? I am not dying.'

The sister picked up the bundle of sweets, dug a hole in the earth and buried it.

'What are you doing?' said the brother. 'Why are you burying my sweets? I was looking forward to eating them when I woke up.'

'Dearest, sweetest brother,' said the sister, 'I accidentally ground a snake in the grain when I was making the sweets. Please forgive me. Why don't you come with me now and I will make some fresh sweets for your journey.'

'I would return with you,' said the brother, 'but my marriage day is drawing near and I cannot delay. However, instead of returning home, why don't you come along with me?'

The sister agreed and, with just the clothes on her back, set off with her brother. The two of them continued on their long journey. Soon they came to a well. The sister wanted a drink of water so the brother said, 'You go ahead to the well and draw some water. I'll just rest here on this embankment.'

When the sister got to the well, she noticed that there was an old stonecutter there, hacking away at a huge rock.

The sister smiled at him sympathetically, offering him a drink of the water that she had drawn and said, 'That is very hard work you are doing.'

'Yes,' said the old stonecutter, 'sometimes one is fated to do hard work. Fate is strange,' he went on, 'look at that young man resting on that embankment.'

The sister was startled but tried not to show it.

'That young man is going through a terrible period. Fate, right now, has nothing good in store for him. He is doomed to die. There is only one way in which he can be saved. If he has a sister—a loving sister—she can save him.'

'How? How?' cried the sister.

'By pretending to be mad and by doing everything contrary to what is expected of her. She should also curse and swear at her brother.'

'For how long must the sister do this?'

'Until his fate changes. And that will only happen after the young man's bride has been in his house for a day.'

The sister then ran towards her brother crying out 'You idiot, you fool, you lout, you son of an owl!'

The brother could not believe his ears. 'What is the matter with you? Until an hour ago, I was your "dearest, sweetest brother" and now you are calling me all kinds of names. You must have gone mad.'

'I may be mad,' yelled the sister, 'but you are a cowardly she-monkey. Come on, come on, let's keep walking or else you'll never get to your stupid wedding to marry your stupid bride.'

The brother just could not understand what had happened to his sister. He thought it best to be quiet.

They walked like this, he quiet, she cursing and rude, all the way to their parents' home.

As soon as they entered the front door, the sister yelled at her brother, 'You sap, you son of a donkey, you pigeon without a tail.'

The mother put her hands to her ears.

'Oh son,' she said, 'your sister has lost her senses. She comes to the wedding in an old, worn-out sari, cursing like a maniac. It would have been best if you had not brought her with you. She is going to ruin this entire wedding. What will all our guests think?'

'Mother,' said the son, 'I don't understand. She was fine . . . for a while. Then I don't know what happened. She just lost her senses when we were halfway here.'

The day of the wedding came. Just as the groom was about to have his wedding crown placed on his head, his sister began screaming, 'Wait. Wait, you numbskulls.' So saying, she began to prod the crown with a needle.

'What *is* she doing?' wailed the mother. 'She is going to embarrass us all.'

The needle was stuck into the crown again and again while the sister giggled hysterically.

Suddenly, a thin viper wriggled out of the crown. Everyone gasped and said, 'His sister may be mad, but at least she has done him some good.'

When the brother mounted the wedding horse that would follow the wedding procession to the bride's house, the sister began yelling again, 'Get my

rotten brother off that rotten horse. I want to ride it. I want to ride it. Get him off.'

She made such a fuss that the family thought the best way to keep her quiet would be to indulge her and let her ride until they were just outside the house. The 'mad' sister got on the horse and just as she was leaving the house, the gateway collapsed on her, slightly hurting her. All the family and guests came running.

'She may be mad,' they said, 'but she has done some good.'

The brother then went off with his wedding procession to marry his bride and all the women of the household waited, as is the custom, in their home.

When the son came back with his bride and was just about to retire to the bridal chamber, the sister began screaming again, 'I want to sleep in that bed. Get my brother and sister-in-law out of here. I must sleep in that flower-decorated bed.'

Again, the family thought, 'She is quite mad, but we had best indulge her or she will keep yelling through the night.'

As soon as the sister lay down on the bridal bed, a large scorpion crawled out of it.

The next day, the mother said to her son, 'Your sister is completely mad. We could lock her up in a back room or we could send her back to her family. Let us just send her back. And why bother to give her that nice gold sari we bought for her as a wedding favour? We will just give her a torn, old sari. She won't even know the difference.'

A whole day had passed since the new bride had come home. The sister now spoke out in her normal, sober voice, 'No, you will not give me the torn, old sari. I deserve the gold sari for all I have been through. An old, wise stone-cutter on the way here told me that my brother's stars were crossed and that the only way I could save his life was by cursing him, by being mad, and by being contrary. I have done all that—and suffered the abuse you have heaped on me. Now I will leave *with* my gold sari. Don't forget:

> With my love
> I have saved a mother's son
> A sister's brother
> And a bride's groom

No, I am not mad. Goodbye to you all!'

NINE DAYS' FESTIVAL

When the snows melt in her Himalayan home, Parvati, Shiva's wife, comes down to visit her mother, Earth, for nine days. For most Indians—and especially for my family—this was a time to bundle together all our year's longings and then present them to the goddess in the form of neat, silent requests.

This was not done crudely. We did not just march up to a statue of Parvati and say 'I want this,' or 'I want that.' We did it properly. We prayed morning and evening, the women fasted, and the poor in one neighbourhood were given food and cooking pots. Parvati herself was offered stuffed breads and halvas, chickpeas cooked with potatoes and lamb stewed without onions and garlic. Parvati was one of the few goddesses that seemed to enjoy eating meat—but not, it seems, onion and garlic.

It was only after Parvati had eaten that we discreetly put in our requests. I might whisper to the goddess that a summer holiday in the Simla Hills would do the family a lot of good or that I wanted to do better than Nash Boga in the next Arithmetic test, or that I would kill myself if I did not get the part of Robin Hood in the school play.

But the best part about the Nine Days' Festival, which came in late March or April, was the stories that were told, one for each day. Here are a few of them.

The Old Man and the Magic Bowl

THE OLD MAN'S LIFE had been hard, but somehow, he had always managed to earn enough to feed himself and his wife.

With the passing years, an awful stiffness had attacked his hands and feet—and then spread with well-aimed cruelty to his legs, arms and back. He could hardly move, let alone go out to work.

He could not pay his rent, so he lost his house and had to live in a hut.

He could not work for a living, so he and his wife began to starve.

When the Nine Days' Festival arrived, the old man felt more depressed than ever.

He was standing listlessly by the roadside when a friend of his passed by.

'Well,' said the friend, 'and how are you today?'

'Not so good,' replied the old man.

'Why, what is the matter?' asked his friend.

'My bones are stiff,' said the old man, 'I have no job and no house. My wife and I have not eaten for seven days.'

'Well,' said the friend, 'if you take my advice . . .'

'Yes?' said the old man.

'My advice is that you go straight to Parvati's temple and throw yourself at her mercy. She is bound to help you. You had better hurry or the festival might end.'

The old man could hardly hurry. With tiny, painful steps, he began the long journey towards Parvati's temple.

It was evening when he got there.

The temple was packed as were all the courtyards that surrounded it. People were spilling out into the streets.

The old man could hear the prayers and smell the far off incense. But he could not get in.

Inside the temple, the goddess Parvati was beginning to feel uncomfortable. She turned to one of her many child-attendants and said, 'Someone's problems are weighing on me like a ton of bricks. Go and find out who is in trouble and bring that person to me.'

Two of the child-attendants flew around the courtyards and into the street. There they spotted the old man standing stiffly under a tree. They circled him once and made a perfect landing at his feet.

'The goddess Parvati summons you,' they chanted together. Each attendant took one of the old man's hands, lifted him off the ground, and then flew him into the temple's innermost chambers. Parvati was leaning casually against a door, her pale, beautiful face radiating as much light as her gold sari.

'Why are you so unhappy?' she asked gently.

'Praise be to you, goddess,' the old man began as he kneeled and touched her feet, 'I have not eaten for several days.'

'Take this,' said the goddess, handing the old man a simple wooden bowl made from the knot in a teak tree. 'Whenever you are hungry, wash the bowl and pray. Then wish for any food that your heart desires.'

'Any food I want and as *much* as I want?' asked the old man.

'Any food you want and as much as you want,' answered the goddess.

The old man wrapped his precious bowl in rags and began the slow walk home to his wife where they hugged each other, marvelling at Parvati's generosity.

The old man said to his wife, 'Now tell me what you want to eat.'

'How about a sweet mango?'

The old man washed the bowl, prayed and then wished for a sweet mango. Before he could even finish his thought, there was the mango sitting in his bowl.

'What else do you want?' asked the old man.

'How about a rice pilaf made with the meat of a fan-tailed sheep?'

'Here it comes,' said the husband. The bowl was soon brimming over with the fragrant pilaf.

'How about a creamy pudding, dotted with raisins?' ventured the wife.

The wooden bowl was now filled with the tastiest pudding the old couple had ever eaten.

'This is a meal fit for a king,' declared the old man.

'It certainly is,' agreed the wife.

The old man began to think. 'You know,' he started, 'all our lives we have been poor. We have hardly had enough food for ourselves, let alone enough food to entertain guests with. Now that we can have all the finest, rarest delicacies of this world, why don't we invite the King for a meal.'

'You must be mad,' said his wife. 'Why should the King come to eat with the likes of us?'

'And why not?' asked the old man. 'He cannot get a better meal anywhere else. We will be offering the King the best food our heavens can provide.'

So saying, the old man set off to invite the King.

When he arrived at the palace gate, the old man said, 'I have come to invite the King to dinner.'

The guards laughed. 'So you want to invite the King? And why not? This might just make his day.'

They led the old man into the King's chamber thinking that the King would enjoy the joke.

The old man joined his palms and bowed respectfully before the King. 'Your majesty, I have come to invite you to my home for dinner.'

The King and all his courtiers began to laugh. Some of the courtiers laughed so hard, they practically doubled up from the effort.

'So,' said the King, 'you, ha-ha-ha-ha, want to invite me to, ha-ha-ha-ha, dinner. Do you want me to come alone or do you want my Queen and courtiers as well?'

'Oh, well,' said the old man, 'your Queen and the courtiers are all welcome.'

'Ha-ha-ha-ha,' laughed the whole court.

Now, the King had quite an evil Prime Minister who added his suggestion: 'What about the army? Aren't you going to invite the whole army?'

'Certainly. The whole army is invited as well,' said the old man.

The King and the courtiers laughed so hard, they did not even notice the old man leave.

The day before the dinner, the evil Prime Minister said to the King, 'Your majesty, would it not be a good idea to check on the old man? Perhaps we should send out some spies to see if dinner for hundreds of thousands is actually being prepared.'

Spies were sent out to the old man's hut. They snooped around for several hours and came back to the palace with this information. 'Your majesty,' they said, 'we saw a large, neat hut in which enough shiny leaf-plates and earthen-ware cups were laid out to feed an entire kingdom. But we did not see any signs of food being cooked. No grain was being ground, no rice was soaking and no vegetables were being stewed in pots.'

'Strange. Very strange,' said the King. 'Now that we have accepted the invitation, we will just have to go and see what the old man has in store for us.'

'And if the food is not adequate, we will cut off the old man's head,' the Prime Minister said viciously.

The next day the King, Queen, courtiers and army set off for the old man's hut.

Carpets had been spread on the floor and all the places neatly laid out. There was no sign of food.

The Prime Minister sniffed. 'I cannot smell any kitchen smells. Strange.'

The old man joined his palms together and bowed before the King. 'Please be seated, your majesties. It was kind of you to come.' He then washed his wooden bowl and prayed. 'Let the King, Queen, courtiers and army get whatever they desire to eat,' the old man commanded the bowl.

Before anyone could move an eyelid, there appeared muskmelons from Central Asia, as sweet as sugar, Persian rice pilaf flavoured with saffron and oranges, pheasants and puddings and creams and stews and halvas. As each man and woman dreamt of a particular food, it appeared in the bowl.

The King and his people were amazed. When dinner was finished, the evil Prime Minister turned to the King and said, 'Such an unusual wooden bowl doesn't really belong with this stupid old man. He can eat any old thing. Even

scraps. It is you—and your court—who should own this treasure.'

As the King's party was leaving, the evil Prime Minister stretched out his hand, saying, 'The King thanks you for your meal and desires that you let him take care of the bowl.'

What could the old man do? He handed over his bowl—and was left to starve again.

Meanwhile, the King put the old man's bowl into one of his many storerooms and forgot all about it.

When the Nine Days' Festival came around again, the old man returned to Parvati's temple and bowed his head in prayer.

'Oh, goddess Parvati, I made such a mistake. I tried to be so grand. I even invited the King for dinner. Now he has taken away the wooden bowl and we are starving.'

Parvati handed the old man a wooden rod and said, 'Take this and whenever you are hungry, wash it, pray and ask for whatever you desire. And do not forget to invite the King to dinner once again.'

The old man did as he was told. He went to the King and asked him to return for another meal. 'Your majesty, I do hope you will not forget your Queen, courtiers and army.'

This time the King and his courtiers did not laugh. But they were curious.

'I wonder what trick the old man has up his sleeve this time?' mused the evil Prime Minister.

Once again, the King sent spies to the old man's hut a day before the dinner. Once again, the spies returned, saying, 'Your majesty, we saw a large, neat hut in which enough shining leaf-plates and earthenware cups were laid out to feed an entire kingdom. But we didn't see any signs of food being cooked. No grain was being ground, no rice was soaking and no vegetables were being stirred in pots.'

'Strange. Very strange,' said the King, 'but we have accepted the invitation and must find out what the old man has in store for us.'

The next day the King, Queen, courtiers and army set out for the old man's hut.

The old man put his palms together and bowed before the King and Queen. 'Please be seated, your majesties. It was so kind of you to come.' He then washed his wooden rod and prayed. 'Let the King, Queen, courtiers and army get whatever they desire,' he commanded the rod.

But instead of producing food, the rod began flying through the air, beating everyone. It beat the King, it beat the courtiers, and most of all, it beat the evil Prime Minister.

'Ouch, ouch, ouch,' they all cried.

'Ouch,' cried the evil Prime Minister.

The King turned to the old man. 'Did you call us to dine or did you call us so we could be beaten?' the King asked. 'What is going on here?'

'I beg your forgiveness, your majesty,' the old man said. 'I did, indeed, invite you for dinner. The fact of the matter is that this rod is the master and the bowl you have is his wife. The rod is in a bad temper because he wants his wife returned to him.'

The King did not want to be beaten any more so he said to his Prime Minister, 'Where on earth is that wooden bowl we took away from the old man?'

'It is probably lying in some storeroom or other,' said the evil Prime Minister, still rubbing himself all over after his beating.

So the King sent off a servant to his storeroom to find the bowl.

It was only after the bowl was returned to the old man that the beatings stopped.

Then the old man washed both the bowl and rod, prayed and said, 'Let the King, Queen, courtiers and army be served whatever foods they desire.'

The best food from heaven was served.

The old man was happy.

So was his wife.

And so was goddess Parvati.

The King
Without
an Heir

I N THE OLDEN DAYS, when kings went out for a ride, all the people they passed had to show respect by joining their palms and bowing their heads. King Rudra was used to seeing nothing but a sea of bowed heads as he took his early morning ride.

One day, something strange happened. As he was passing a river bank, a washerman who was scrubbing his clothes on a board, suddenly stopped work, stood up his board, looked the King straight in the eye and spat on the ground.

The King was startled, but being good-natured, he decided to say nothing and ride on.

The next day, the same thing happened. When the King passed the riverbank, the same washerman stopped work, stood up his board, looked the King straight in the eye and spat on the ground.

This continued for a whole week with the King saying nothing. On the eighth day, the King could bear it no longer. He stopped his horse and addressed the washerman. 'Look here,' he began, 'for seven days you have been insulting me. This is ridiculous. What is the reason for this?'

'Forgive me, your majesty,' the washerman said. 'You are an unlucky man. You are an unlucky man because you have no heir. It cannot do me any good to look upon the face of an unlucky man first thing every morning. So I spit, hoping that my luck will not be as bad as yours.'

King Rudra did not like hearing this at all but he had no answer for the washerman. Although he was, indeed, childless, he was still quite young and he had not given the matter much thought.

Now, of course, he could think of nothing else. Did the whole kingdom think of him as the unlucky king? Would they all begin to spit whenever he appeared in public? The thought made him wince.

By the time he got home, he was so depressed that he went straight to his bedroom and lay down.

Queen Rukmani, his wife, came to his chambers and asked, 'Why is your majesty so sad? What can be troubling you?'

'Oh, nothing at all,' answered the King.

'*Something* must be the matter. You haven't washed and you haven't eaten. This is not like you at all.'

'Well, since you ask, I'll tell you,' the King said. And he went on to relate the story of his meeting with the washerman.

The Queen seemed quite understanding. 'There *is* a solution to the problem, you know. Why don't you marry my younger sister, Chandini. Perhaps you will be luckier with her.'

So the King married Queen Rukmani's younger sister. But the new marriage failed to produce an heir. The King was more depressed than ever.

One day Queen Rukmani and Queen Chandini came to the King's chambers and said, 'Why is your majesty so depressed? You haven't washed and you haven't eaten. This is not like you at all.'

So the King said, 'This is ridiculous. I have two queens now and still no heir. The public will soon start spitting at me.'

'There is a solution to this problem,' said Queen Chandini. 'Why don't you marry my younger sister, Shalini. Perhaps you'll be luckier with her.'

The King married Queen Shalini—but his bad luck continued. On the advice of his wives, he even married the remaining sisters, Rohini, Kamini, Padmini and Damini. Still, no heir was born.

By this time, the King was quite fed up with his wives. He called his Chief Minister and said, 'This is ridiculous. I have married seven wives and still I don't have a child. I am thoroughly disgusted with the seven Queens. Why don't you take the pack of them and lock them up in the attic. Leave a sack of roasted chickpeas for them to eat. They certainly do not deserve better.'

So the queens were locked up in the attic. They were not too happy about this. Here they were, wives of a mighty ruler, locked up with nothing better than cattle fodder.

The oldest of them, Queen Rukmani, said, 'Matters have got out of hand. There must be a solution to this problem. We must organize. We must think.'

They had a conference. The youngest, Queen Damini, said, 'I have a thought. Why don't we tell the King that I am expecting a baby?'

'But you are *not*,' said Queen Chandini quite logically. 'We would be telling a lie.'

'I know, I know,' said Queen Damini. 'But it would give us time to work something out. Meanwhile, we won't have to be locked up in the attic and left to eat roasted chickpeas for dinner day after day.'

'She has a point,' said Queen Rukmani, who hated roasted chickpeas. 'Get me some writing parchment.'

Queen Shalini ran to get some writing parchment and a quill.

Queen Rukmani wrote, 'My dearest Lord, it is with great pleasure that I wish to inform you that your youngest wife, my youngest sister, Queen Damini, is with child. Her condition is quite delicate. It would be best if she were removed to more comfortable and familiar surroundings.'

When the King got the note, he began to jump up and down with joy. 'This is ridiculously wonderful!' he cried.

All the Queens were allowed to return to their chambers. Queen Damini was sent a message saying that the King wished to see her immediately.

Instead of Queen Damini, the person who came to see him was Queen Rukmani.

'My dearest Lord,' she began, 'your youngest Queen is in a delicate state. It would not do to get her excited. It is best if you wait until the baby is safely born.'

'Oh, yes, of course,' agreed the King. 'Do you need a doctor or a midwife?'

'Please do not worry. We will take care of mother and child ourselves. After all, we are so many of us, all sisters.'

The months passed by in relative peace.

Everyday, the Queens tied new bandages on to Queen Damini's stomach to make it appear to 'grow'. Then they sent her for a walk in the garden so the King could see her from a distance.

When the King became restless, they patted his arm, saying, 'Any day, any day now.'

One day Queen Rukmani came to the King with the long-awaited announcement, 'Your majesty, a son has been born.'

The King began to dance. 'This is wonderfully ridiculous. Ridiculously wonderful. Give sweets to everyone in the palace. To everyone in the kingdom. Now, when can I see my prince?'

'Not yet,' advised Queen Rukmani. 'His health is delicate.'

'But I haven't even heard his cries!'

'You will, you will,' said his eldest Queen.

Inside the Queens' chambers, a goat kid had been brought in. Queen Damini tweaked its ear and it cried, 'Ma-a-a!'

'See,' said Queen Rukmani to the King, 'your baby is crying, don't disturb it.'

Every day the Queens would hang nappies out to dry, and every now and then they would tweak the goat kid's ear to make it cry.

Six months passed this way. It was now time for the Nine Days' Festival. The Queens knew that their only hope lay with goddess Parvati.

The King let the Queens know that he was going to go to Parvati's temple with *all* his wives *and* his son.

Queen Rukmani said to the King, 'Oh, yes. We shall all go. The Queens and the baby will travel in curtained palanquins. We don't want you to forget the special offering for the goddess—the gold umbrella that we have had made.'

When the procession of the King and Queens reached the temple, the eldest Queen turned to the King and said, 'I have left the golden umbrella at home. We cannot possibly go into the temple without an offering. Perhaps you had better return and fetch it.'

The poor King had to go all the way back to the palace for the umbrella.

Meanwhile, the Queens all jumped out from their curtained palanquins and rushed inside the temple.

There they threw themselves at the feet of goddess Parvati, saying, 'Help

us, help us get out of the mess we are in. We know we have lied. But if we do not produce a child, we will just die of shame.'

Parvati took a lump of halva and formed a baby. Then she sprinkled a little blood and a little holy water on it. Soon the baby was breathing and crying.

'It is mine,' said Queen Rukmani.

'It is mine,' said Queen Chandini.

'It is mine,' said Queen Shalini.

'It is mine,' said Queen Rohini.

'It is mine,' said Queen Kamini.

'It is mine,' said Queen Padmini.

'It is mine,' said Queen Damini. 'It was my idea in the first place.'

All the Queens began to fight over the baby. 'Enough,' said the goddess Parvati. 'Enough of this squabbling. All of you, put on humble blouses made out of sack-cloth with simple ties of rope. Then stand facing the sun. Only one of you has breasts that will produce milk. *That* is the mother of this baby.'

Suddenly fine streams of milk began spouting from Queen Damini's breasts. She bent down to claim her child.

Just then the King returned with the golden umbrella. 'This is ridiculous. I don't see why I had to go all the way. . .' Then he stopped.

There, holding a sweet little boy, was Queen Damini. 'This is wonderfully, wonderfully ridiculous,' said the King. 'My heir, I have an heir. No one will spit on me. Let us all go into the temple and thank the goddess Parvati.'

Only the Queens knew just how much they had to thank Parvati for!

The Girl
in the
Forest

ONCE UPON A TIME, there was a girl who lived alone in a forest. She did not know her parents for they had died when she was little. There was not much to eat in the forest except roots and leaves, so the girl depended upon the charity of passing strangers who often gave her roasted grains of millet and barley from their knapsacks.

It just so happened that although the girl was poor, she had been graced with the most exquisite face and body.

One misty dawn, it chanced that a rich, handsome King came riding through this forest. As his horse was racing towards the red morning sun, the King saw a brilliant glimmer moving behind the leaves. He eased his horse cautiously towards it.

If the horse moved a step, so did the glimmer. If the horse stopped, so did the glimmer.

The King was very puzzled. He got off his horse and called, 'Who is it?'

There was no answer. The King wondered if he was being deceived by a sunbeam.

As he moved closer to the glimmer, it streaked through several bushes and moved away. The King ran after it.

When he stopped again, so did the glimmer, but this time, the King could hear quick, shallow breathing.

'Come out of there. I order you to come out of there,' the King called.

Again, the glimmer began moving with great speed. The King chased it and when he was close enough to hear the same shallow breathing, he jumped upon it.

To his great surprise, the King found himself holding a young, beautiful maiden in his arms.

Her long hair fell behind her like a sheet of silk, her eyes, large and soft, were gazing at him like a frightened deer.

'Do not be frightened, beautiful princess,' the King said in soothing tones. 'All I want to do,' went on the King, quite overcome by her beauty and proud bearing, 'is to ask you to marry me. Will you please marry me?'

The young maiden had been equally struck by the King. 'Oh, yes,' she answered, 'yes, yes.'

The King lifted her up onto his horse and then jumped up behind her. Together they rode towards his palace where a solemn marriage ceremony was performed.

A year passed. One day, the Queen called her handmaidens and said, 'For breakfast today, I would like some grains of roasted millet and barley.'

The handmaidens were astonished. Only poor peasants ate roasted grains of millet and barley, but they thought royalty had strange ways and off they went to the market to buy the required grains.

As the Queen was sitting nibbling at her breakfast, the King chanced to come to the door.

'Whatever are you eating?' he asked.

The Queen put her plate behind her, shielding it from the King's eyes, and answered, 'Pearls . . . just pearls.'

The King was silent for a moment. 'Wherever did you get such a large collection of pearls?'

'Oh,' she answered, trying to sound casual, 'they were sent to me by my parents. This is what I was used to eating for breakfast at home.'

The King said, 'In our home, my dearest Queen, we might serve saffron rice cooked with raisins or roasted deer or dates stuffed with walnuts, but never pearls. Your father's home must be so much grander than ours. I am sure you must miss it. I would very much like to take you back to visit your parents. We can leave tomorrow.'

Terror struck at the heart of the Queen. She ran to goddess Parvati's temple and fell at her feet. 'Oh Parvati,' she prayed, 'save me! save me! I do love my husband so very much. I never told him I was a princess. He just assumed

I was. I was far too afraid to correct him lest he leave me. And when he came in and saw me eating roasted grains of barley and millet, I was at my wit's end. I lied out of panic. Please, please, help me.'

Parvati felt sorry for this good, kind Queen and said, 'For three hours I will give you just the kind of home that your husband expects to see. I will give you a father and a mother and all necessary relatives and servants. For three hours only.'

The Queen thanked Parvati and rushed back to the palace where arrangements were already being made for a visit to the Queen's ancestral home.

The next day the royal party—with horses, palanquins and servants—set out at dawn. The Queen guided them through the forest until they reached a clearing. 'There,' she said, pointing to a distant castle, 'there is my father's palace.'

The palace exceeded all the King's expectations for it was made entirely of gold. The doors and windows were made from gleaming rock crystal edged with emeralds. There was a large bathing pool outside, which was studded with sapphires right down to its coolest bottom. In the garden there were arbors where juicy grapes hung in luscious bunches and mango trees laden with their sweet fruit. Musicians strolled about playing lutes, horns, conch shells and two-sided drums.

A sumptuous feast had been laid out like a picnic on the grass. Standing around it were liveried servants, shooing away flies with peacock feathers and yak-tail fans.

'Welcome to our home,' said the Queen's gracious parents. 'Would you like to bathe in our pool before we settle down to eat?' they asked the King.

Now the King had already been struck by the blue waters of their unusual pool. He thanked his hosts and changed into his bathing loincloth.

'This has been the most refreshing experience of my life,' he said as he came out dripping with water. Attendants helped him dress and hung up his wet loincloth to dry on a bush.

The next hour was spent in eating roasted quail from golden plates and drinking orange blossom wine from hollowed out rubies.

Dusk fell. The Queen began to urge the King to return home.

'Why so early, my Queen?' the King said, 'I'm really enjoying myself. Your parents have been so kind and hospitable. I would like to get to know them better.'

'Perhaps some other time,' the Queen said, 'I do feel we have stayed long enough.'

'Couldn't we just spend a week here? Don't you enjoy being home?' the King asked.

'Oh, yes I do,' answered the Queen, now near tears, 'but . . . I feel . . . we shouldn't . . . be a burden to my old parents.'

'All right, my sweet,' said the King, 'if you insist on returning then we will but we should visit your parents again. This place is a true paradise.'

And so the King's party returned home.

The following day, the King realized that he had left his wet loincloth drying on a bush. He called one of his courtiers and asked him to send a couple of horsemen with gifts for the Queen's parents and with instructions to collect the loincloth.

The horsemen headed towards the Queen's father's palace. But when they neared the clearing from which they had spotted the palace, they saw nothing.

'The day is a bit hazy,' one horseman said, 'perhaps it is a bit further ahead.' On and on they went without any sign of the palace.

'This seems to be just about where the palace should be,' said the second horseman.

'Quite obviously, you are wrong,' said the first horseman. 'Perhaps we took a wrong turning.'

'I just don't see where we could have made a mistake,' said the second horseman.

Just then, on a very familiar bush, beside a simple pond, they saw the King's loincloth. It was dry now and fluttering gently in the breeze.

The horsemen folded it neatly and returned to their King. There, they told their story adding, 'Your majesty, it is exceedingly strange. We saw a pond and a bush, but no jewelled palace, no garden, no musicians, and no liveried servants.'

The King went to his Queen and said, 'I cannot understand this. My horsemen have just returned with the loincloth I left drying in your father's garden.'

The Queen let out a gasp.

'But,' went on the King, 'they saw no golden palace, no sapphire-lined pool, no musicians, no. . .'

'Please don't go on,' said the Queen, falling down in a heap. 'Oh, forgive me. I have no father or mother. I lived all alone in the forest when you met me. What you saw me eating was not pearls but roasted grains of barley and millet. I did not mean to deceive you. I was so afraid of losing you that what I blurted out . . . was a lie. And then, when you wanted to visit my family, I appealed to goddess Parvati for help. The golden palace, the sapphire-lined pool, that was all the goddess' doing. She helped me out. Please, find it in your heart to forgive me.'

The King embraced his wife and said, 'There is nothing to forgive. You did what you did out of love. If goddess Parvati understood your predicament, who am I to complain? Perhaps we should go to Parvati's temple together and offer her our thanks.'

THE FESTIVAL FOR PARVATI

Shortly after the Nine Days' festival, came Gungaur. Again, we celebrated the virtues of goddess Parvati, who as my mother explained, could take many forms. She could turn her tongue black and develop fangs, she could ride bravely on a tiger or, if she wished, she could give off glory and warmth like the sun.

I liked Parvati best in her glorious form, the form she took at Gungaur. My mother would collect us all in her prayer room and ask, 'So, which Shiva-Parvati story would you like to hear today?'

Shiva was Parvati's huband—and the Creator and Destroyer of the Universe besides. The god and goddess loved each other so much that whenever a human couple seemed particularly devoted to each other, my mother would smile and say, 'How nice—they are just like Shiva and Parvati.'

At Gungaur, we could pick any Shiva-Parvati story that we liked. My favourite had to do with the birth of their fat, roly-poly, elephant-headed son, Ganesh.

My mother would start by putting her open hands on either side of her face and flapping them.

'Ganesh has big ears, so he can hear everything,' she would say.

Then, she would stretch one arm in front of her nose and wave it.

'Ganesh has a big trunk of a nose so he can smell everything.'

My mother would then rub her stomach and add, 'And Ganesh has a big tummy so he can digest the most intricate, complicated thoughts.'

After this little introduction, the story would start.

How Ganesh
got his Elephant Head

SHIVA, THE MIGHTY GOD with the blue throat, lives high up in the Himalaya Mountains with his beautiful wife, Parvati. Sometimes, life is not much fun for her, for Shiva is often away for years at a time on his usual business of creating and destroying people and dancing on top of the world to keep it going.

On one occasion Parvati did not know when he might return. She was bored. There was not much she could do all by herself on a mountain peak, and she was feeling exceedingly lonely. It suddenly occurred to her that she was, after all, a goddess and could do whatever she wished. What she needed was a playmate . . . not a playmate that would annoy Shiva, as his anger could be deadly in more senses than one, but a sweet, innocent playmate . . . Parvati kept thinking along these lines. Finally, the perfect solution dawned on her.

'I will make myself a baby,' she cried with happiness, 'I will make myself a baby boy.'

Parvati found some clay and water. She pounded the clay until it was soft and pliable and then she began to shape a baby. The first form she made looked too ordinary and not cuddly enough. So she began to add clay to its stomach until it was fat and round. Parvati laughed to herself. She was beginning to love the baby already.

Parvati then took her right forefinger and poked it into the baby's stomach to make a belly button. 'Oh, it is going to be a lovely baby,' she said to herself.

She put the baby in the sun to dry. Soon it opened its eyes and began to smile. Parvati was overjoyed. She had found the perfect playmate.

Everywhere Parvati went, she took her baby. She cooed to it, talked to it and spent many hours laughing at its antics.

Several years passed this way. One day, Parvati took her son for a long walk. They were both quite tired and when they came to a pool of water Parvati wanted to stop and bathe in it, but she felt shy about being seen by a passerby. So she said to her son, 'Could you please be my guard? Don't let anyone come near the pool while I am bathing.' The roly-poly boy sat down upon a large flat stone while his mother made her way into the refreshing water.

Now, it so happened that Shiva had just finished dancing on a mountain top and was returning home. He heard some splashing in a pool and knew

that it had to be his wife. He was about to walk towards the water when he found himself stopped by a fat little boy.

'Don't go any further,' the boy ordered.

Shiva was not used to taking orders. He tried to brush the boy aside but the boy resisted and fought back. Shiva's anger began to mount. His throat became bluer and the veins in his forehead began to swell and throb. Suddenly, without warning, Shiva drew out a sword and cut off the boy's head.

Parvati, hearing a commotion, slipped into her clothes and rushed towards Ganesh. She let out a scream and fell sobbing to the ground.

Shiva watched in amazement. He realized that he had done something terrible but did not know what it was. He apologized, hoping that would calm his wife, and then asked her what he had done to upset her so.

'It's your vile temper,' she answered.

'But,' he said, 'you knew about my temper when you married me. Surely that is not what is upsetting you *now*!'

'You have murdered our child.' Parvati was quite hysterical by now.

'Our child?' asked Shiva. This was the first he had heard of a child.

'You never understand anything,' Parvati screamed. 'You stay away for years and years on distant mountain tops. You don't care what happens to me.'

Shiva did not seem to understand.

'You said that I had killed our child. But we have no child!'

'Of course we have,' Parvati said. 'We have a child because I made one. I made one because I was lonely. I was lonely because you were away. Of course we have a child. I should say that . . . we . . . *had* . . . a . . . child.

The pieces in the puzzle suddenly locked into place. Shiva was so sorry that he begged his wife to tell him what he could do to redeem himself.

Parvati said, 'Go out into the forest with your mighty sword. I want you to cut off the head of the first living creature you see and bring it back. Fit the head on our child and give it life. That is what I want. If you do not do this for me, I will never speak to you again.'

Even though Shiva's work took him away for long periods, he did love his wife and did not want to lose her. So he did as he was told. He went into the forest with his mighty sword, looking for a living creature.

Well, the first living creature he saw was an elephant. Shiva cut off its head and dutifully brought it home. He fitted the head on to the child's body, breathing life into it as he did so, and waited for his wife's reaction.

To his surprise, Parvati was enchanted. She stroked the child's trunk and declared that this boy was even better than her first creation.

Shiva sighed with relief. By now, he was beginning to get very fond of the child himself. . .

Dear Reader,

The last of the year's stories has been told. The hot summer winds will blow again, sending us flying in search of shade from kindly banyan trees. There will be compensations, of course. The same sun that will burn our skins will ripen our mangoes and fill them with the sweetest juice. We will throw these mangoes into tubs of ice and later feast on them. The watermelons will swell in the sandy fields across the Yamuna River and other children will learn to swim with them. The cycle of stories will start again, some new ones to remind us that we do not know everything, and some old ones to teach us that our values are constant. The world will be different next year. But it will also be the same.

Love,
Madhur Jaffrey

Who is Who, What is What, and a Guide to Pronunciations

Quite a few of these stories have been taken from the Hindu epics, the Ramayan and the Mahabharat, both of which were written before the birth of Christ.

As far as pronunciation is concerned, you almost cannot go wrong if you give equal emphasis to every syllable in an Indian word. There are some letters of the alphabet that may be unfamiliar. There are, for example, a soft 'd' and 't', both of which are said by hitting the tip of the tongue against the back of the top front teeth.

The pronunciations suggested here are those in popular use throughout much of North India.

Amrit (Am/rit) 'Am' rhymes with 'mum'; 'rit' rhymes with 'bit', only the 't' is soft. Amrit is the nectar of immortality. One single sip of this liquid provides eternal life.

Aya (A/ya) 'A' rhymes with 'ma'; 'ya' also rhymes with 'ma'. An aya is an Indian nanny who looks after children.

Ayodhya (A/yodh/ya) The 'A' is like the 'A' in America; 'yodh' rhymes with 'slowed' (the 'dh' is pronounced as if you were saying the 'dh' in 'mud house', only the 'd' is soft); 'ya' rhymes with 'ma'. This ancient city once existed on the banks of the Saryu River in what is Uttar Pradesh today. It was the capital of the powerful Kosala kingdom.

Balram (Bal/ram) 'Bal' rhymes with 'dull'; 'ram' rhymes with 'calm'. Balram was Krishna's older brother. Some people believe that he was really a foster-brother, the son of Krishna's aunt and uncle, Yashoda and Nanda. Others believe that he was a true brother and that he was also spirited away from prison, just like Krishna, and raised by his aunt and uncle.

Bharat (Bha/rat) The 'bh' sound does not exist in English. Say 'club house'—that is the 'bh' sound; the 'a' in 'Bha' is like the 'u' in 'but'; 'rat' rhymes with 'but', only the 't' is soft. Bharat was the son of King Dashrat and Queen Kaikeyi and Ram's half-brother.

Chandini (Chand/in/i) The 'a' in 'Chand' is like the 'a' in 'calm'—the 'd' is soft; 'in' rhymes with 'sin'; the final 'i' has the 'ee' sound as in 'bee'. She is a fictional character, the second wife of King Rudra.

Chanur (Cha/nur) 'Cha' rhymes with 'ma'; the 'u' in 'nur' is like the 'oo' in 'boo'. Chanur was a wrestler employed by the wicked King Kans. He was killed by Krishna.

Damini (Da/min/i) 'Da' rhymes with 'ma'—the 'D' is soft; 'min' rhymes with 'tin'; the final 'i' has the 'ee' sound as in 'bee'. She is a fictional character, the seventh and youngest wife of King Rudra.

Dandaka (Dan/dak/a) 'Dan' rhymes with 'bun'; 'dak' rhymes with 'buck'—the 'd' is soft; the final 'a' is like the 'A' in 'America'. Dandaka Forest lies between the Narmada and Godavari rivers in the present-day states of Madhya Pradesh and Maharashtra. When Ram was banished from his kingdom, he and his wife Sita had many adventures in this forest.

Dashrat (Dash/rat) 'Dash' rhymes with 'hush'—the 'd' is soft; 'rat' rhymes with 'hut'—only the 't' is soft. King Dashrat was Ram's father. You will notice that he appears in two stories, Shravan Kumar and his Wife and How Ram Defeated the Demon King Ravan. In the first story he is cursed and in the second story the curse comes true.

Devaki (Dev/a/ki) 'Dev' rhymes with 'save'—the 'd' is soft; the 'a' is like the 'A' in 'America'; 'ki' is pronounced like 'key'. Devaki was the mother of Krishna, the wife of Vasudev and the sister of the wicked King Kans.

Divali (Div/a/li) 'Div' rhymes with 'give'; the 'a' is like the 'a' in 'calm'; 'li' rhymes with 'bee'. Divali is the Festival of Lights that takes place on a moonless night in the late autumn. Little oil lamps (now candles and electric bulbs) light up homes both to please Lakshmi, the goddess of wealth and prosperity and to welcome Ram back to his rightful kingdom after fourteen years of exile.

Doda (Do/da) 'Do' rhymes with 'go'; 'da' rhymes with 'ma'—both 'd's are soft. Doda, the thoughtful brother, is probably a fictional character.

Dodi (Do/di) 'Do' rhymes with 'go'; 'di' rhymes with 'bee'—both 'd's are soft. Dodi, the loving daughter and sister, is probably a fictional character.

Dussehra (Dus/seh/ra) 'Dus' is said rather like 'thus'—the 'd' is soft; the 'e' in 'seh' is like the 'e' in 'bet'; 'ra' rhymes with 'ma'. This festival falls on the tenth day of the waxing moon around late September. It celebrates the victory of the good King Ram over the demon Ravan.

Ganesh (Gan/esh) 'Gan' is said just like the word 'gun'; the 'e' in 'esh' is like the 'a' in 'lake'. Known as the god of wisdom and the remover of obstacles, Ganesh is the son of Shiva and Parvati. He has the head of an elephant.

Gaya (Ga/ya) The 'g' is like the 'g' in 'go'; the 'a' in the first syllable is like the 'u' in 'but'; 'ya' rhymes with 'ma'. A town in Bihar and known since very ancient times as a place of pilgrimage for Hindus.

Gokul (Go/kul) 'Go' is said just like the English word 'go'; 'kul' rhymes with 'bull'. A village in Uttar Pradesh, not far from Mathura.

Gungaur (Gun/gaur) The two 'g's are said like the 'g' in 'go'; the 'u' in 'gun' is like the 'u' in 'put'; the 'au' in 'gaur' is like the 'o' in 'or'. The festival of Gungaur, which falls on the third day of the waxing moon in the early summer, celebrates the virtues of the goddess Parvati in her form as Gauri, the Brilliant and Glorious.

Hanuman (Han/u/man) 'Han' rhymes with 'bun'; the 'u' is pronounced like the 'oo' in 'boo'; the 'a' in 'man' is like the 'a' in 'calm'. Hanuman, the monkey god, was a brave chieftain in the Kingdom of Monkeys and Bears somewhere in Southern India. He became Ram's friend and ally and helped him to find the abducted Sita.

Hiranya Kashyap (Hir/an/ya Kash/yap) The 'i' in 'Hir' is like the 'i' in 'bit'; the 'an' is just like the 'un' in 'until'; 'ya' rhymes with 'ma'. 'Kash' rhymes with 'hush'; 'yap' rhymes with 'cup'. Hiranya Kashyap was the wicked king who thought he was God. He was even willing to have his son, Prahlad, killed for believing in a more Heavenly Almighty.

Holi (Ho/li) Pronounced just like 'holy'. This is the Indian Spring Festival when winter crops are harvested. It was the custom during Krishna's time to celebrate the festival by throwing coloured water and coloured powders on friends and strangers alike. The same custom is followed today. Some of the new crops are also burned as an offering to God.

Holika (Ho/lik/a) 'Ho' rhymes with 'bow'; 'lik' rhymes with 'sick'; the 'a' is said like the 'a' in 'calm'. Holika was Hiranya Kashyap's sister and Prahlad's aunt. She got burned in the fire that was intended for her nephew.

Indrajit (In/dra/jit) 'In' rhymes with 'bin'; 'dra' is just like the 'dra' in 'Hydra', only the 'd' is soft; 'jit' rhymes with 'beat', only the 't' is soft. Indrajit was the son of Lanka's demon king, Ravan. He was killed by Ram's half-brother, Laxshman.

Janak (Jan/ak) 'Jan' rhymes with 'bun'; 'ak' rhymes with 'buck'. King Janak, who lived well before Christ, ruled over the kingdom of Mithila in northern Bihar. He was the father of Ram's wife, Sita.

Kaikeyi (Kai/ke/yi) The 'ai' sound is like the 'a' sound in 'dare'; the 'e' in 'ke' is like the 'u' in 'but'; 'yi' rhymes with 'bec'. Kaikeyi was King Dashrat's third and youngest queen, the mother of Ram's half-brother, Bharat.

Kaliya (Kal/i/ya) The 'a' in 'Kal' is like the 'a' in 'calm'; the 'i' is said like the 'i' in 'bit'; 'ya' rhymes with 'ma'. Kaliya was a wicked serpent king with five heads who dwelt in the deep pools of the Yamuna River. He was killed by Krishna.

Kamini (Ka/min/i) 'Ka' rhymes with 'ma'; 'min' rhymes with 'bin'; the 'i' is like the 'ee' in 'bee'. A fictional character and the third wife of King Rudra.

Kans (Kans) 'Kans' rhymes with 'dunce'. King Kans was Krishna's wicked uncle. Krishna eventually killed him.

Karva (Kar/va) The 'a' in 'kar' is like the 'u' in 'but'; 'va' rhymes with 'ma'. The karva pot, made out of terra-cotta, is symbolic of the married woman. It has a spout and lid and looks like a small, round-bottomed tea-pot. The 'exchanging' of karva pots can only take place between two married women and consists, not of actual exchanges but of symbolic tilts in each others direction.

Karvachauth (Kar/va/chauth) The 'a' in 'Kar' is like the 'u' in 'but'; 'va' rhymes with 'ma'; the 'au' in 'chauth' is like the 'ou' in 'bought'—the 'th' sound is closest to the 'th' in 'think'. This is the festival that falls on the fourth day of the waning moon around October when married women fast and pray that God gives long life to their husbands.

Kaushalya (Kau/shal/ya) The 'au' sound in 'Kau' is like the 'a' in 'all'; 'shal' rhymes with 'dull'; the 'ya' is pronounced just 'ya' to rhyme with 'ma'. Kaushalya was King Dashrat's eldest queen and Ram's mother.

Korma (Kor/ma) 'Ko' rhymes with 'go'; 'ma' rhymes with 'pa'. Generally an Indian meat dish with a creamy sauce containing yoghurt.

Kosala (Ko/sal/a) 'Ko' rhymes with 'go'; 'sal' rhymes with 'dull'; the 'a' at the end is like the 'A' in 'America'. According to Hindu literature, the kingdom of Kosala was one of the great powers in north India from about 700 B.C. to at least about 500 B.C. It was in Uttar Pradesh and could have extended further south and east. The capital of Kosala was Ayodhya. Its most famous ruler was Ram.

Krishna (Krish/na) 'Krish' rhymes with 'wish'; 'na' rhymes with 'ma'. Krishna lived before Christ. He is worshipped in India as he is thought to be an incarnation of the god Vishnu. He is the hero of an ancient Indian epic, the Mahabharat, where he is shown as a wise philosopher, a trustworthy friend, a brave warrior, and an irresistible lover.

Lakshmi (Laksh/mi) The first syllable is pronounced 'Lucksh'—i.e. 'luck' with an 'sh' added on; 'mi' rhymes with 'bee'. Lakshmi is the goddess of wealth and prosperity.

Lanka (Lank/a) 'Lank' rhymes with 'dunk'; the final 'a' is like the 'a' in 'calm'. Lanka was the ancient name for the island nation just south of India that was once called Ceylon and is now called Sri Lanka.

Laxshman (Laxsh/man) The first syllable is pronounced 'Lucksh'—i.e. 'luck' with an 'sh' added on; 'man' rhymes with 'bun'. Laxshman was Ram's younger half-brother, the son of King Dashrat and Queen Sumitra and the twin of Shatrughan.

Masoom Ali (Ma/soom A/li) 'Ma' rhymes with 'pa'; 'soom' rhymes with 'boom'; the 'A' is like the 'A' in America; 'li' rhymes with 'bee'. He was one of my grandfather's chauffeurs when I was little.

Mathura (Math/u/ra) The 'a' in 'Math' is like the 'u' in 'but'—the 'th' sound does not exist in English but is closest to the 'th' in 'think'; the 'u' sounds like the 'ou' in 'could'; 'ra' rhymes with 'ma'. Mathura, a holy city of many temples, is on the bank of the Yamuna River in Uttar Pradesh. It is the birthplace of Krishna.

Mustik (Mus/tik) 'Mus' rhymes with 'bus'; 'tik' rhymes with 'lick'—the 't' is soft. Mustik was a wrestler employed by King Kans. He was killed by Krishna's brother, Balram.

Nanda (Nan/da) 'Nan' rhymes with 'bun'; 'da' rhymes with 'ma'. Nanda was Krishna's uncle and Yashoda's husband. Since he raised Krishna from infancy, he is often referred to as Krishna's father.

Neem (Neem) 'Neem' rhymes with 'seem'. A neem tree is exceedingly shady. Its bitter but medicinally potent, twigs are used as a combination of toothpaste and toothbrush. Its fruit, though inedible, is good for medicines.

Padmini (Pad/min/i) 'Pad' rhymes with 'dud'—only the 'd' is soft; 'min' rhymes with 'tin'; the final 'i' is like the 'ee' in 'bee'. A fictional character and the fifth wife of King Rudra.

Parvati (Par/vat/i) 'Par' rhymes with 'bar'; the 'a' in 'vat' is like the 'u' in 'but'—the 't' is soft; the final 'i' is like the 'ee' in 'bee'. Parvati is the wife of Shiva and the daughter of the Himalaya Mountains. She is a goddess who can take many forms, from gentle to bloodthirsty. She can be called an Earth Mother (as she is in the story of Karvachauth) or Devi (as she is during the Nine Days' Festival) or Gauri as she is at Gungaur.

Pootana (Poot/a/na) 'Poot' rhymes with 'boot'—only the 't' is soft; the 'a' is like the 'A' in 'America'; 'na' rhymes with 'ma'. Pootana was a wicked demon. She tried to kill the infant Krishna by disguising herself as a wet nurse and putting poison on her nipples.

Prahlad (Prah/lad) The 'a' in 'Prah' is like the 'a' in 'bank'; the 'a' in 'lad' is like the 'a' in 'calm'—the 'd' is soft. Prahlad was the son of Hiranya Kashyap. Unlike his father, he was a devotee of God. His father tried, unsuccessfully, to have him killed for this very reason.

Rahu (Ra/hu) 'Ra' rhymes with 'ma'; 'hu' is said just like the English word 'who'. Sometimes called a planet and at others the King of Meteors, Rahu is known chiefly for causing the eclipse of the sun and moon.

Ram (Ram) 'Ram' rhymes with 'calm'. Ram lived before Christ and is the hero of the ancient Hindu epic, the Ramayan. Born as a prince and an heir, he eventually inherited the kingdom of Kosala in Uttar Pradesh. His father was King Dashrat and his mother Queen Kaushalya. Sita was his wife. Ram was just, honest, honourable and a brave warrior. He is worshipped in India as he is thought to be an incarnation of the god Vishnu.

Ravan (Ra/van) 'Ra' rhymes with 'ma'; 'van' rhymes with 'bun'. Ravan was the wicked demon king of Lanka (now called Sri Lanka). He had ten heads and twenty arms and was eventually killed in battle by Ram.

Rohini (Ro/hin/i) 'Ro' rhymes with 'bow'; 'hin' rhymes with 'tin'; 'i' rhymes with 'bee'. A fictional character and the fourth wife of King Rudra.

Rudra (Rud/ra) 'Rud' rhymes with 'could' only the 'd' is soft; 'ra' rhymes with 'ma'. This is a fictional character. King Rudra had seven queens, all sisters.

Rukmani (Ruk/man/i) 'Ruk' rhymes with 'book'; 'man' rhymes with 'ton'; 'i' rhymes with 'bee'. A fictional character in my story, the first wife of King Rudra.

Sa'ab (Sa'ab) The two 'a's together are pronounced like the 'a' in 'calm'. Sa'ab is the short form of 'sahib' which is a term of respect, rather like 'sir'.

Saryu (Sar/yu) The 'a' in 'sar' is like the 'u' in 'but'; 'yu' is pronounced just like the English 'you'. The River Saryu flowed beside the ancient town of Ayodhya in what is now the state of Uttar Pradesh.

Satyavan (Sat/ya/van) 'Sat' rhymes with 'but'; the 'a' in 'ya' is like the 'o' in 'come'; the 'a' in 'van' is like the 'a' in 'calm'. Satyavan is a mythological figure—the good woodcutter who married the good princess, Savitri.

Savitri (Sa/vit/ri) 'Sa' rhymes with 'ma'; 'vit' rhymes with 'sit'; 'ri' rhymes with 'bee'. Savitri is a mythological figure who symbolizes wifely devotion. She was the princess who married Satyavan, a poor woodcutter.

Shalini (Sha/lin/i) 'Sha' rhymes with 'ma'; 'lin' rhymes with 'tin'; 'i' rhymes with 'bee'. A fictional character and the third wife of King Rudra.

Shatrughan (Shat/ru/ghan) 'Shat' is said very much like 'shut' only the 't' is soft; 'ru' rhymes with 'blue'; there is no 'gh' sound in English—try saying 'big *h*ouse' and then you will get the 'gh' sound—'ghan' rhymes with bun. Shatrughan was Ram's younger half-brother, the son of King Dashrat and Queen Sumitra and the twin of Laxshman.

Shiva (Shiv/a) 'Shiv' rhymes with 'give'; the final 'a' is like the 'A' in 'America'. Shiva, also called Mahesh, is part of the Hindu trilogy of gods, Brahma, Vishnu and Shiva. Shiva both destroys life and re-creates it (Brahma creates it, Vishnu preserves it). Shiva has a blue throat, four arms and sometimes five faces. He does the dance of creation over the world to keep it spinning.

Shravan Kumar (Shrav/an Ku/mar) 'Shrav' rhymes with 'dove'; 'an' rhymes with 'bun'; the 'u' in 'Ku' is like the 'ou' in 'could'; 'mar' rhymes with 'bar'. Shravan Kumar was the good son of blind parents who was accidentally shot by King Dashrat. He often symbolizes a son's devotion and sense of duty towards his parents.

Sita (Si/ta) 'Si' rhymes with 'bee'; 'ta' rhymes with 'ma'—the 't' is soft. Sita was Ram's wife and King Janak's daughter. She was good, kind, honourable and quite devoted to her husband.

Sugreev (Su/greev) The 'u' in 'Su' is like the 'ou' in 'could'; 'greev' is pronounced exactly like 'grieve'. Sugreev, a monkey, was the king of the Kingdom of Monkeys and Bears in what is now thought to be a region of Mysore. He was dethroned by his brother but later won his kingdom back with the help of Ram and his friend, the monkey chieftain, Hanuman.

Sumitra (Su/mit/ra) The 'u' in 'Su' is like the 'u' in 'put', 'mit' almost rhymes with 'bit', only the 't' is soft; 'ra' rhymes with 'ma'. Sumitra was King Dashrat's second wife and the mother of the twin princes, Laxshman and Shatrughan. The twin boys were Ram's half-brothers.

Vasudev (Va/su/dev) 'Va' rhymes with 'ma'; 'su' rhymes with 'do'; 'dev' rhymes with 'save'. Vasudev was Krishna's father and Devaki's husband.

Vishnu (Vish/nu) 'Vish' rhymes with 'dish'; 'nu' rhymes with 'boo'. Vishnu is part of the trilogy of Hindu gods, Brahma, Vishnu and Shiva. Vishnu preserves life (Brahma creates it, Shiva destroys it and can re-create it). Hindus believe that Vishnu reincarnated himself in both Ram and Krishna.

Yamraj (Yam/raj) 'Yam' rhymes with 'hum'; the 'a' in 'raj' is like the 'a' in 'calm'—the 'j' is like the 'j' in 'jam'. Yamraj is the King of the Underworld and the God of the Dead.

Yamuna (Yam/u/na) 'Yam' rhymes with 'mum'; the 'u' is said like the 'oo' in 'book'; 'na' rhymes with 'ma'. The Yamuna River is a tributary of the Ganges River. It starts in the Himalaya Mountains and flows along the cities of Delhi, Mathura and Agra to join the Ganges at Allahabad.

Yashoda (Yash/o/da) 'Yash' rhymes with 'hush'; the 'o' rhymes with 'no'; 'da' rhymes with 'ma'—the 'd' is soft. Yashoda was Krishna's aunt, his father Vasudev's sister and Nanda's wife. Since she raised Krishna from infancy, she is often referred to as Krishna's mother.

Acknowledgements

I wish to express my deep thanks to the many members of my very large family who have helped me. It was Prem Bhua who started me off, and Kiran Bhua and Shammo Bhua who kept supplying the missing pieces. I would like to thank my bhabi, Asha (who in turn consulted her father, Kash Bhua and her sister) for her methodical and invaluable research, Brijda for looking up moon-days in the almanac, Inder Bhabi and Suneeta for providing strategic support, Kattojiji for putting up with my intrusive tape-recorder not once but twice and for feeding me *karhi* and rice into the bargain, Bina for directing me to Kattojiji, Asha (of Asha-Rama) for being generous with her memories and for taking a gerbil off my hands, and Zia for her painstaking assistance with the proofs.

I would also like to thank the Department of Tourism, Government of India, as well as the External Affairs Ministry Government of India for their invaluable help.